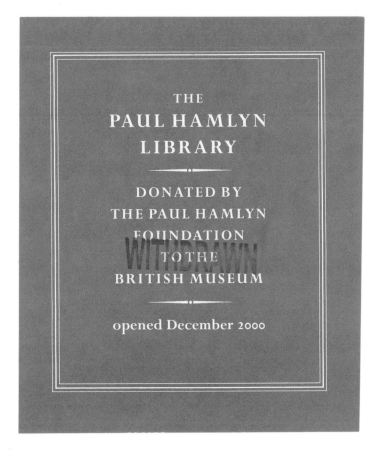

THE
ATLAS *of*
Endangered
PEOPLES

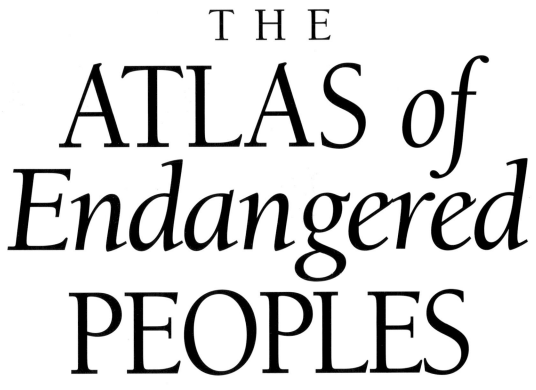

Belitha Press

First published in the UK in 1995 by
Belitha Press Limited
31 Newington Green, London N16 9PU
Copyright in this format © Belitha Press 1995
Text copyright © Steve Pollock 1995
Illustrations copyright © Belitha Press 1995
Cartography copyright © Creative Cartography 1989
Black and white illustrations by Cat & Mouse Design Consultants, London
Miniature maps by Eugene Fleury
Editor: Neil Champion
Designed by Cat & Mouse Design Consultants, London
Consultant: Steve Watts
Printed in Singapore for Imago

ISBN 1 85561 360 3

Picture acknowledgements: BBC Education Photo Library: 20 bottom and 23
top Luke Finn; Bruce Coleman Ltd: 18 bottom John Cancalosi, 56 top Johnny
Johnson; Hulton Deutsch Collection: 54 bottom left; Hutchison Library: 34
bottom right Sarah Errington, 38 top, 40 top Anatoly Pashouk, 52 top Bruce
Wils; Images of India Picture Agency: 44 bottom and 45 centre Roderick
Johnson; Magnum Photos Ltd: 30 bottom James Nachtwey, 49 bottom Ian
Berry; NASA: 58 top; Planet Earth Pictures: 58 bottom Norman Cobley;
Popperfoto: 28 bottom and 49 centre; Nick Saunders\Barbara Heller: 7 top
and 54 top; Science Photo Library: 16 bottom right CNRI, 20 top Hank Morgan,
24 bottom Astrid and Hanns-Frieder Michler, 38 bottom George Bernard, 54
bottom right US National Archives; Frank Spooner Pictures: 4 bottom, 5 right,
8 bottom, 9 top, 16 top and bottom left, 22 centre and bottom, 23 centre,
24 top, 36 both, 40 bottom, 42 bottom, 45 bottom, 50 bottom and 52 bottom;
Still Pictures: cover, title page, 4 top, 6 bottom, 7 bottom, 8 top, 10, 14 both,
18 top, 34 bottom left and 44 top Mark Edwards, 6 centre and 17 top Paul
Harrison, 9 bottom Herbert Girardet, 17 bottom John Maier, 22 top Joseph
Rodriquez/Mira Bildarchiv, 26 top and 28 top Andre Maslennikov, cover and 26
bottom Hans Huidebang/Samfoto, cover and 30 top Teit Hornbak/2Maj, 32 top
Teit Hornbak, 32 bottom Heldur Metocny, 34 top Jorgen Schytte, 35 top Ole
Bernt Frøshaug/Samfoto, 35 bottom Romano Cagnoni, 42 top Bios, cover,
46 bottom and 48 bottom Rahul Sengupta/2Maj, 48 top Fred
Friberg/Samfoto/2Maj, 50 top Nigel Dickinson, 56 bottom B & C Alexander.

CONTENTS

INTRODUCTION

▲ *Fresh vegetables on a market stall in Bolivia.*

There are threats to human life all over the world in different shapes and forms. These threats include war, pollution, disease, hunger, poverty and displacement. At present there are around 5 billion people on Earth, and the number increases every day. This in itself is a problem. Our success as a species has led to over-population in some areas of the world and this is the cause of many of the environmental problems that we face in the world today.

PROBLEMS WITH PROGRESS

One of the main reasons for the success of human beings has been our increasing ability to control and change the environment. We have learned how to grow more grains, vegetables, fruits and meat; we mine for ores and coal and drill for oil; we build homes, offices and factories, roads and airports. But change brings problems as well as benefits. Cutting down trees on mountain slopes may cause landslides and floods in towns and villages in the valleys (for example, in Bangladesh). Oil spills are a major form of pollution. Pesticides and fertilisers help us grow more food, but can harm food chains and eventually poison the soil. Factories produce the goods we want, but some pollute the air.

AN UNEQUAL WORLD

Many people want to make their lives more secure and comfortable and to become more rich and powerful. But this has not happened at the same rate in all countries. There are differences between the way of life in developed and developing countries (see box). The world's resources are used much faster by industrialised countries. But about twice as many people live in the developing world as in the developed world.

▼ *Rescue workers search for bodies after a landslide in a poor area of Colombia, South America.*

DEVELOPED AND DEVELOPING

These words are used to describe countries or regions that have either strong or weak **industrial economies**. They are often linked with other terms which describe their economies. The word 'developed' is linked with industrial, first world and north, and 'developing' with rural, third world and south. The last word in each group (north/south) tells you roughly where these countries are. Countries in the northern hemisphere are usually developed and industrial, but countries in the southern hemisphere are usually developing and rural.

Poverty is a serious problem in the developing world, and this makes many of the other problems that people face much worse.

This book describes the conditions in which people live in different parts of the world. It looks at why people still go hungry and die of curable diseases despite amazing progress in science and technology. The book also looks at why people are forced to leave their homes, or are persecuted and sometimes even killed by other people.

PEOPLE EVERYWHERE

About 250,000 people are born worldwide every day at present. There are just over 90 million new mouths to feed every year. This is equivalent to the entire population of Mexico. Ninety per cent (more than 80 million) of these births are in developing countries, where over-population is already a serious problem.

Today many people live longer because of improved medicine and this makes matters worse. The result in poorer countries is high unemployment, fast-spreading slums, less effective education and healthcare, and inadequate sanitation and drinking water. The growth in population in developing countries will not slow down until everyone living in these countries has certain basic necessities such as these.

RURAL-URBAN MIGRATION

Fifty years ago only one in 100 people lived in a city of over a million inhabitants, and 99 people out of 100 lived in towns, villages or in the countryside. Today, ten times the number live in large cities. By the year 2010 more people will live in towns and cities than in the countryside.

The developing countries are changing most. People living in the countryside cannot find jobs and do not have enough land to grow food to feed themselves or their families. So they move to the cities in the hope of finding work. This is called rural-urban migration and it happens all over the developing world. When people arrive from the countryside there is nowhere for them to live. They

▲ Contrasting buildings in Sao Paulo, Brazil.

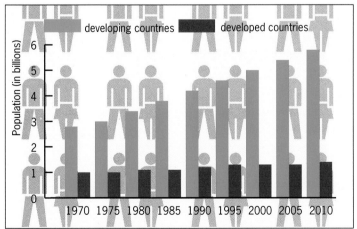

▲ How the population has grown and will continue to grow in developed and developing countries.

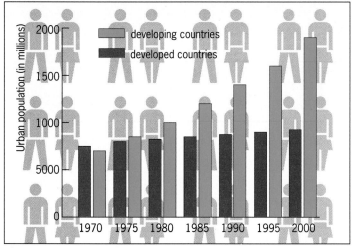

▲ *How many people will live in cities by the year 2000*

make simple shelters on the outskirts of the city. When millions of people do this in one place they create shanty towns with appalling living conditions. The people living in these shanty towns have no sanitation and no access to clean water. Their makeshift houses are built from scrap materials. These living conditions are bad for their health. Often shanty towns are built on land that nobody else wants because it is too damp, too steep for

proper building or, in some cases, polluted.

In some countries the people in charge of the city have tried to pull these shanty towns down, but the people just build them again because they have nowhere else to go. In other countries the city authorities have helped to improve shanty towns by putting in drains, electricity, roads, clean water and by helping to build proper houses.

Whatever happens, more and more people will migrate in this way. On the outskirts of Mexico City one shanty town called Netzhuacoyotl has 2 million inhabitants. By the year 2000 there will be 26 million people living in Mexico City.

▲ *Whole families like this one spend three months of each year picking coffee in Guatemala.*

HEALTH AND DISEASE

Throughout the world there is a link between money and health. Poorer people are less likely to have clean water to drink, or acceptable kinds of sanitation. They may live in areas where there are diseases such as malaria and river blindness. Being poor means they cannot afford the drugs which treat the disease, or prevent it from becoming a problem. Sometimes babies and young children become ill because of the poor conditions in which they are brought up. These children may die from a simple illness such as diarrhoea because their parents do not have the salts and sugars they need to keep them alive while they are ill.

In poor conditions diseases spread rapidly so that many more people suffer or die than is necessary. Often **vaccination** programmes can prevent diseases spreading or from turning into **epidemics**. But many countries cannot afford to buy the necessary vaccines and have to rely on outside aid and support.

▲ *Too many people and not enough room in Dhaka.*

Throughout the centuries indigenous peoples (see page 9) have been badly treated by other peoples, such as explorers or settlers, who have invaded and taken over their land and natural resources. Sometimes whole civilisations have died out, such as the Aztecs in Mexico and the Incas in South America. When the Spanish invaders came they brought with them diseases to which the Spanish had built up a natural **immunity**. Childhood diseases, such as measles, killed many people because they had no previous contact with them. Many thousands of people died. This still happens today, when contact is made between people from cities who live with a disease, and native people, who have not been exposed to it before.

◀ A drawing of the Spanish fighting the Incas done in 1565 and found in Peru early this century.

REFUGEES

Refugees are people who are forced to leave their homes. There may be several reasons for this. Drought caused hundreds of thousands of people to leave their homes in the Sahel Region in Africa. Many died looking for food and water.

War is another cause. The war in Afghanistan made one in four people a refugee. Some people are persecuted for belonging to a particular religious or ethnic group and forced to move. When life becomes too unbearable or too dangerous for people they often become refugees.

In some developing countries fewer and fewer people are allowed enough land to grow their crops. Richer landowners buy more land to grow cash crops which they sell to make money. Small farmers have to choose between unemployment in a big city or trying to live off too little land. They often cut down

▲ A health worker injects a villager in Bangladesh.

virgin forest and use the land the trees were growing on to raise crops.

About 150 million people are cutting down tropical forests all over the world to make a living in this way. These people are refugees. The lives of the people who live in the forests also come under threat. Sometimes they are forced off their lands and then they become refugees too, with nowhere to go. This is a common problem throughout the developing world. Many of the problems are caused by the way that developing countries are dependent on selling and trading with developed countries.

NORTH–SOUTH TRADE

In most developing countries there is enough land to grow food to feed the whole population. But much of that land is used to grow cash crops, such as coffee, cotton and tobacco. These are sold on the world market, raising money for the growers and the country. Developing countries use most of this money either to buy goods from other countries or to help pay off debts to world banks. This is why they are known as cash crops. People living in the countryside rarely benefit. Any money left over goes first to improving city life.

These countries suffer the most if people's taste for a certain crop changes, or if more of the crop is grown than people can use. If several countries decide to give up valuable land to grow tobacco, for example, and there is a good harvest of the crop around the world, there may be too much grown.

The price the farmers are paid goes down and the countries which grow the crop earn less money to spend on the goods and food that the country needs

▲ *Workers picking tea on a plantation in Indonesia.*

to feed its people. When countries have grown crops to sell on the **world market** and prices have become too high, perhaps because of a shortage, the developed countries may look elsewhere for a cheaper and more reliable supply. This happened in the case of sugar cane, a crop which many developing countries grow for world consumption. When some countries in the developed world started growing sugar beet as the source of their sugar, the price of sugar cane dropped.

In parts of South America sugar cane is no longer grown for food but turned into alcohol and used as fuel to run cars and lorries. Similarly, if smoking or taking sugar become unfashionable, then the earnings of the people of the countries which produce these crops falls.

DISASTERS

People all over the world have suffered the consequences of natural disasters such as earthquakes, volcanic eruptions, or hurricanes. Such events happen very quickly and leave a trail of devastation behind them.

More recently there have been other disasters that at first seem to be natural but are connected with human activity. There was drought in parts of Africa in the mid-1980s. This was because much of the land had been overgrazed by cattle and goats. The trees had been cut down and the land was over-farmed so

▲ *Natural disasters such as this flood in Dhaka, Bangladesh, cause great hardship for people.*

▲ Oil wells on fire in Ahmadi, Kuwait.

that the soil blew away altogether. These conditions make drought more dangerous and the lives of the people in the region more desperate.

Accidents in factories and industrial sites are another type of disaster. In these accidents it is nearly always the poorest people who suffer, because their living conditions are so poor, or because they live very close to polluted and industrial areas.

POLLUTION

Some disasters are more difficult to detect and more long term than others. Pollution of the environment by chemicals happens all the time to a greater or lesser extent. When pesticides were first used, for example, no one realised that they would remain in the environment and become dangerous. Even worse are the many chemicals that are released into the atmosphere by factories, power stations and vehicle exhausts. These chemicals can pollute and alter the air we breathe and, over time, may change the temperature of the Earth.

THE TEN DEADLIEST EARTHQUAKES, 1960-90		
DATE	COUNTRY	NUMBER OF DEATHS
27 July 1976	China	242 000
31 May 1970	Peru	67 000
7 December 1988	CIS	25 000
4 February 1976	Guatamala	22 778
16 September 1978	Iran	20 000
9 February 1960	Morocco	13 100
19 September 1985	Mexico	10 000
10 April 1972	Iran	5 400
23 December 1972	Nicaragua	5 000
24 November 1976	Turkey	3 626

INDIGENOUS PEOPLES

Indigenous is a term used to describe people who are the original inhabitants of an area. These include aborigines in Australia, Maoris in New Zealand, native American Indians and the tribal peoples who live in the rain forests.

Indigenous peoples are often the victims of progress. They have spent thousands of years living in balance with their environment. Today most have had their way of life and their culture changed radically by development. They are losing their identity in an increasingly technological world.

▲ A Kayopo warrior from the Amazon in Brazil.

The beliefs of indigenous peoples in the spirits of the environment around them have been replaced by materialistic progress. New diseases have killed many people in every community. Even today, when many tribes are protected after years of persecution, indigenous peoples continue to lose their land to others who force them to become landless refugees. Often these people prefer to live apart from the society that governs the country they live in, so they have no one to speak for them and are easily persecuted.

LAND STRUGGLES

Indigenous peoples need plenty of land to lead their lives in the traditional way. Their needs often conflict with the needs of others, such as farmers, miners and road-builders. And land, whether for growing crops or mining minerals or to develop in some way, is what people all over the world want. People who lead a **hunter-gatherer** lifestyle need plenty of space. They do not control their surroundings and they do not attempt to change them. They work with

▲ *The Yanomami prepare land for growing vegetables.*

their environment, taking nuts, berries, roots and herbs as they need them and when they can be found. They hunt animals and birds as well. This is how some Australian aborigines, the San of the Kalahari desert in Africa, the pygmies in central Africa and a handful of other tribes around the world still live. They spend less time getting their food than the people in a settled farming community. But they need plenty of land on which to find it.

CULTIVATORS

Some indigenous peoples are **cultivators** and live in settled communities. Unlike hunter-gatherers, cultivators change their environment. They plant root crops such as manioc, yams and sweet potatoes. On the same site they may also plant beans, maize and banana-like plants called plantain.

Some tribal people carry out shifting cultivation. This is particularly common in tropical forests. They burn part of the forest and use the ash as a natural fertiliser. After a few years, when the soil loses its fertility or becomes overgrown with weeds, the people move on to another part of the forest and do the same thing. The soil may not be fertile for 20 years or more after this. So even a small group of shifting cultivators needs a large area of forest in which to live.

Some tribal cultivation is more permanent. Settled communities usually grow up in places where the soil doesn't become easily exhausted. People grow crops and store them. Groups within the community often share jobs such as weeding, planting, harvesting and watering.

Where the land or environment is unsuitable for agriculture, such as in mountainous or very cold regions, people have developed a different way of life.

People who live in traditional communities in these conditions herd animals such as cattle, sheep and goats in Asia and Africa, or llamas and alpacas in South America.

Indigenous people have always had to work with their environment and know how to ensure that it will continue to provide what they need in the future. People in developed countries have developed a way of life which causes much more environmental damage. They practise intensive agriculture. This means that they use large quantities of artificial chemical fertilisers and pesticides in order to grow food for their large populations. Crop yields are increased but at a cost: the chemicals can remain in the soil and build up to harmful levels.

HOW TO USE THIS ATLAS

At the beginning of each entry in this book there are two or three symbols. Each symbol represents something which threatens the health, livelihood or existence of people in that area of the world. There are 21 symbols altogether. They also appear on the maps to show where the people described live. In some cases symbols are included on the map which are not included in the text. Indigenous peoples of the world are included throughout the atlas. There are many more groups of indigenous peoples at risk than the book has space to include.

 CASH CROPS Crops such as coffee, cotton or tobacco, grown to be sold abroad. They bring in money, but use land which could be used for food.

 INDUSTRIALISATION The process by which countries use raw materials to make goods to sell. They use the money to buy things from outside. Industrialisation often leads to pollution and health problems.

 STARVATION Many people starve when their food supply is cut off by war or a natural disaster.

 OPPRESSED PEOPLE Some people such as minority groups suffer at the hands of other people. Minority groups are people who are fewer in number than others around them.

 PEOPLE VERSUS NATURE Nature reserves help the environment and the animals and plants that live there. In national parks the environment and people live side by side. People can be at risk when nature is considered more important.

 DROUGHT Areas which have less rainfall than usual may suffer from drought. People cannot grow enough food to eat. There is not enough water for their animals. The soil becomes dry and light and may blow away.

 HIGH TECH DEVELOPMENT Many industrialised countries have advanced technology. They may use this technology unsuccessfully in developing countries. Large dams are built to provide power which may never be used, and leave people without land.

 REFUGEES People become refugees when their living conditions become so bad that they are forced to leave their homes.

 INDIGENOUS PEOPLES Indigenous peoples are the original inhabitants of an area. They may be persecuted by other people who want to colonise or farm the land they live on.

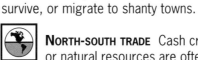 **LANDLESS FARMERS** People without land or jobs have no means of earning a living. They may live in the same way as tribal people to survive, or migrate to shanty towns.

 NORTH-SOUTH TRADE Cash crops or natural resources are often sold by the developing world to the developed world. Less land is available for local farmers to grow their own food.

POLLUTION Manufacturing and intensive agriculture often create pollution. This damages the environment and the health of local people.

WAR When people fight over land, resources or power, the fight often turns into a war. People are often killed or forced to leave.

POLITICAL CHANGE Every country has a government which decides what happens. Changes in government policy affect people's day-to-day lives and some may suffer.

 SHANTY TOWNS. Shanty towns grow up when people move to cities to look for work. They settle at the edge of cities and build makeshift homes.

SOCIAL PROBLEMS People live in different conditions. Poor people often have to live and work in unhealthy conditions, and send their children to work in order to feed their families.

DRUGS Some people use illegal drugs to alter their mood. They may become addicted to them. This puts their health at risk.

 POPULATION The number of people who live in an area or country.

 HUMAN DISASTERS Accidents caused by human error can cause floods, landslides and oil spills.

 DISEASE Sickness is spread by infection, poor sanitation and poor living conditions.

 NATURAL DISASTERS Natural events such as earthquakes put people's lives at risk, destroy their homes and damage the environment.

OTHER FEATURES OF THIS ATLAS
Each large map uses different colours to show types of landscape and symbols to give you more information about a place:

Mountain	Game reserve
Forest and scrub	National park
Desert	Capital city
Arable land	Important town or city
Frozen desert (snow, ice)	Mountain peak

Each large map has other features. A locator map shows where in the world that area is. Also a compass tells you where that area is in relation to north, south, east and west. A ruler tells you the scale of the map – that is, how many kilometres one centimetre across the map equals. They also have lines of latitude and longitude. These imaginary lines are used to divide the world into small areas and are measured in degrees.

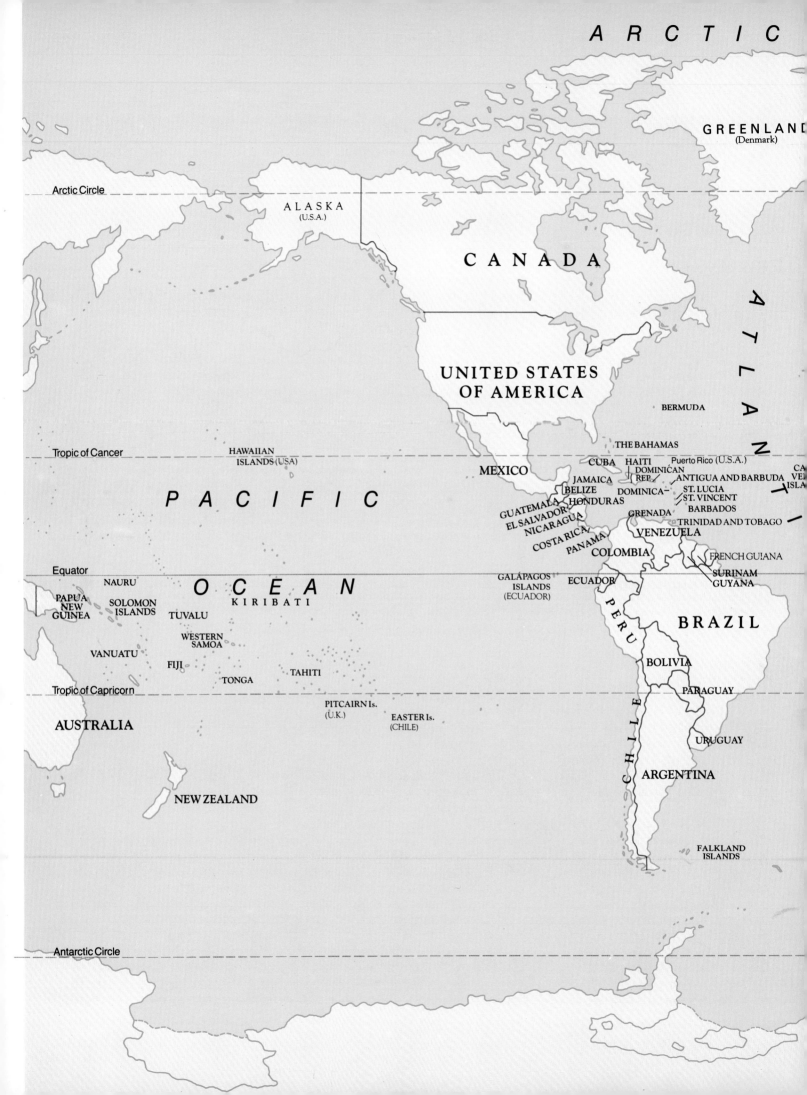

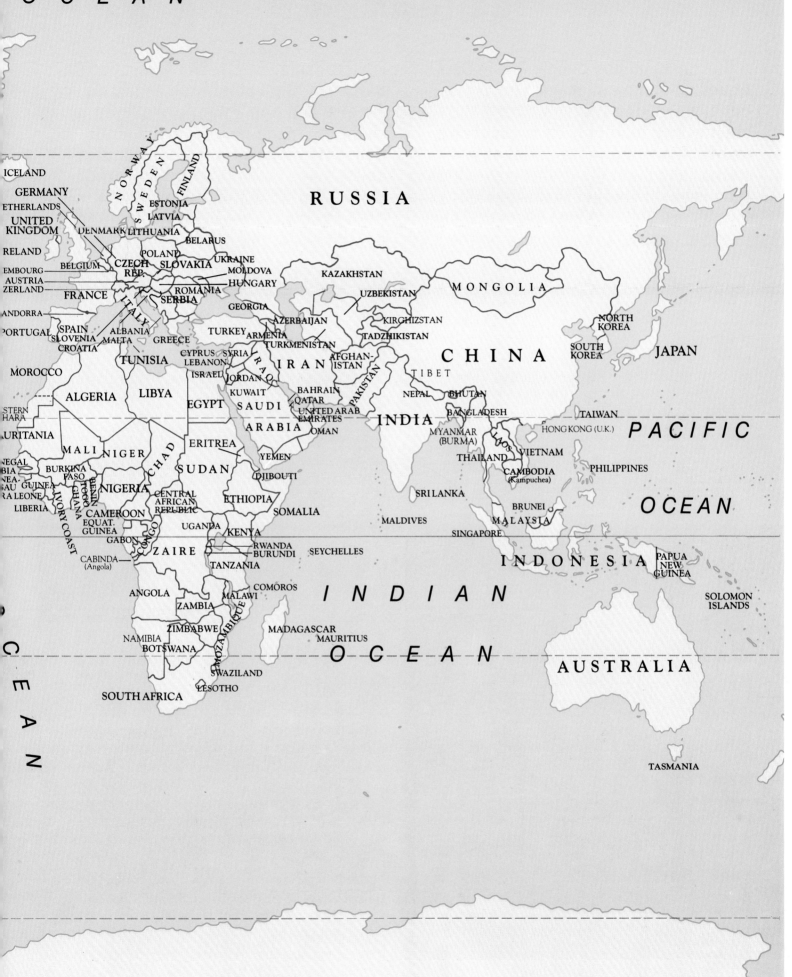

OCEAN

ICELAND
GERMANY
ETHERLANDS
UNITED
KINGDOM
RELAND
EMBOURG   BELGIUM
AUSTRIA
ZERLAND
FRANCE
ANDORRA
PORTUGAL   SPAIN
SLOVENIA
CROATIA

NORWAY   SWEDEN   FINLAND
ESTONIA
LATVIA
DENMARK LITHUANIA
BELARUS
POLAND
CZECH   SLOVAKIA   UKRAINE
REP.   MOLDOVA
                HUNGARY
ROMANIA
SERBIA
ITALY
ALBANIA
MALTA   GREECE

RUSSIA

KAZAKHSTAN

MONGOLIA

UZBEKISTAN
                        KIRGHIZSTAN
GEORGIA
AZERBAIJAN   TADZHIKISTAN
TURKEY   ARMENIA
        TURKMENISTAN   NORTH
                                KOREA
CYPRUS   SYRIA   AFGHAN-
LEBANON   IRAN   ISTAN   CHINA   SOUTH   JAPAN
TUNISIA   ISRAEL JORDAN IRAQ   TIBET   KOREA

MOROCCO   PAKISTAN

ALGERIA   LIBYA   EGYPT   KUWAIT   BAHRAIN   NEPAL   BHUTAN   TAIWAN
                        SAUDI   QATAR   BANGLADESH
STERN   ARABIA   UNITED ARAB   PACIFIC
HARA   EMIRATES   INDIA   MYANMAR   HONG KONG (U.K.)
URITANIA   OMAN   (BURMA)
                    ERITREA   LAOS
MALI   NIGER   CHAD   YEMEN   THAILAND   VIETNAM
NEGAL   SUDAN   OCEAN
BIA   BURKINA   DJIBOUTI   CAMBODIA   PHILIPPINES
NEA-   FASO   SRI LANKA   (Kampuchea)
AU GUINEA   NIGERIA CENTRAL   MALDIVES   BRUNEI
RA LEONE   AFRICAN   ETHIOPIA   MALAYSIA
LIBERIA   CAMEROON REPUBLIC   SINGAPORE
        IVORY COAST EQUAT.   UGANDA   KENYA
                GUINEA   GABON   RWANDA   INDONESIA   PAPUA
                    CONGO   ZAIRE   BURUNDI   SEYCHELLES   NEW
        CABINDA   TANZANIA   GUINEA
        (Angola)   SOLOMON
                ANGOLA   MALAWI   COMOROS   INDIAN   ISLANDS
                        ZAMBIA   OCEAN
                        ZIMBABWE   MADAGASCAR   MAURITIUS
                    NAMIBIA BOTSWANA   MOZAMBIQUE   OCEAN   AUSTRALIA
                                SWAZILAND
                            LESOTHO
                    SOUTH AFRICA   TASMANIA

OCEAN

ANTARCTICA

SOUTH AMERICA

Almost 300 million people live in South America, and most speak Spanish or Portuguese. The region's most outstanding feature is its tropical rain forest. There are more varieties of animal and plant life in this environment than in any other in the world. The forests are still home to many thousands of tribal people. But pressure on the land is increasing, both in the forests and in the cities. Big cities, such as Rio de Janeiro and Sao Paulo, are skirted by shanty towns (called *favellas*). Poor people flood in from the surrounding countryside to live there. They are looking for work, but there is not enough work for everyone. People without jobs or land suffer the most.

▼ NATIVE PEOPLES

Many different tribal groups live in the rain forests and mountains of South America. For hundreds of years they lived as hunter-gatherers or shifting cultivators. Many were wiped out by the new diseases that Europeans brought with them in the sixteenth century. More recently, their environment and way of life has been threatened by miners looking for coal, oil, gold and other minerals. People building roads, or moving in to farm the land are also a threat to these peoples.

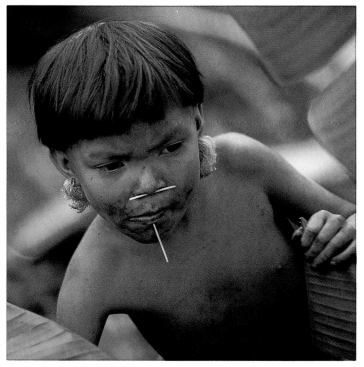

▲ YANOMAMI

This tribal group lives in the Serra Parima in an area known as Roraima in the Amazon rain forest. In 1985 there were about 20,000 of them; but their numbers have decreased to between 5,000 and 9,000 today. Diseases such as malaria are bringing them to the brink of extinction.

There are about 45,000 miners living on the Yanomami's land, looking for gold. They use high-pressure water jets to blast away the river beds in their search for the precious ore. This silts up the rivers and kills the fish the Yanomami eat.

One solution to these sorts of conflict (which happen throughout South America) is to provide protected land for the tribespeople.

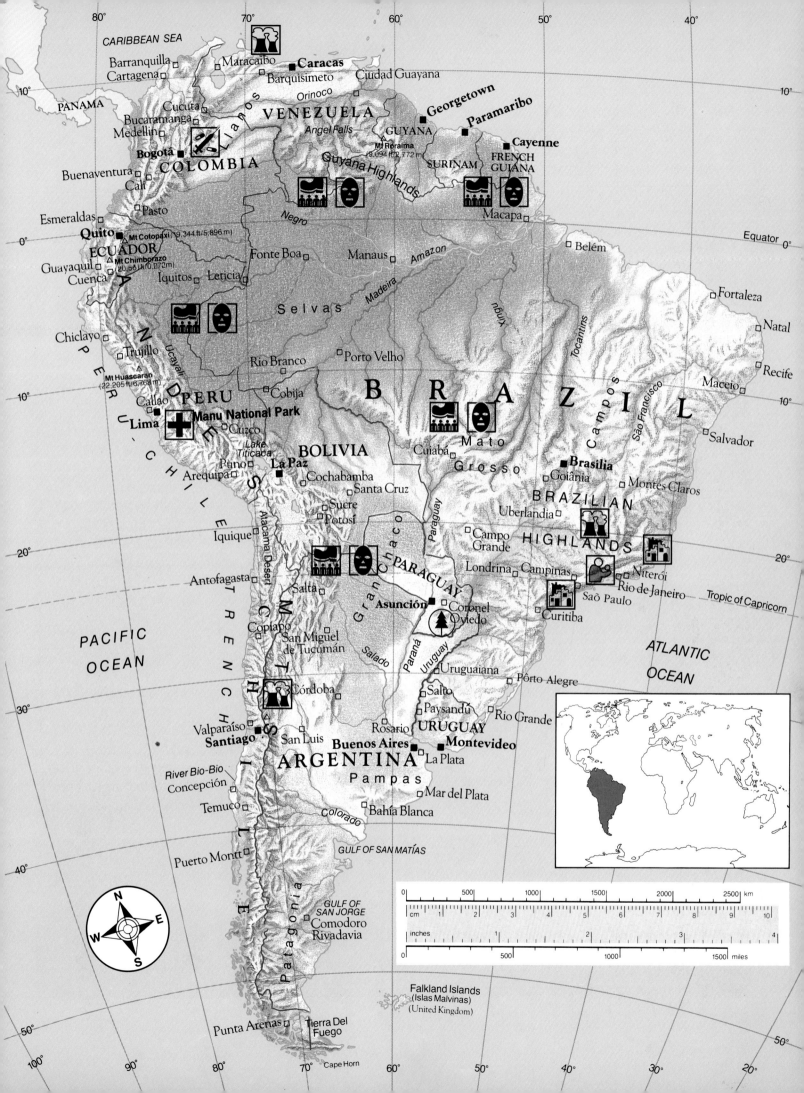

A DRUG PROBLEM

Colombia has a perfect climate for growing two crops – coffee and marijuana. Like many cash crops (see page 7) grown in the developing world, the price of coffee can vary. In good years when a lot of coffee is harvested, prices fall and so does the income the country earns from its coffee. Many people have turned to growing plants which are made into illegal but money-earning drugs. Colombia has also become the main place where people go to buy and sell another drug – cocaine. This is grown in Bolivia and Peru. The drug trade earns large sums of money for a few people in the country. But the cost of living is much higher for ordinary people. This means that small farmers are sometimes forced into growing illegal crops just so they can survive.

▼ CHICO MENDES

This Brazilian rubber tapper was murdered in 1989 because he dared to stand up to the powerful ranchers who were and still are cutting down the rain forests. Mendes took the side of the local tribespeople and brought the world's attention to the violent attacks they were suffering. He became a victim himself.

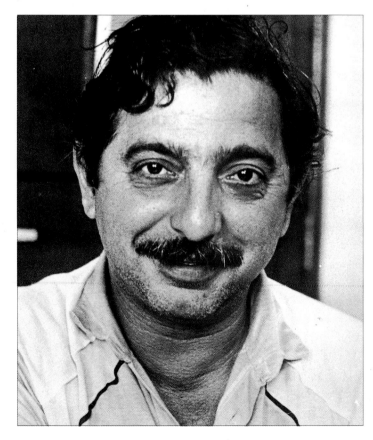

▼ CHOLERA

This deadly disease is carried in water and is extremely infectious. The symptoms of cholera are diarrhoea and vomiting, which cause people to lose liquid and salts from their bodies. Vaccination against the disease, using dead bacteria, has only a limited effect. South America had not suffered from cholera for a hundred years.

But then an epidemic struck in Peru in 1991. The disease spread quickly, killing thousands of people. This disease is made worse by the sort of conditions in which poor people live. Where people are overcrowded, do not have clean drinking water, or have inadequate sanitation cholera spreads more easily. Throughout the world today about 120 million people are at risk from this disease alone.

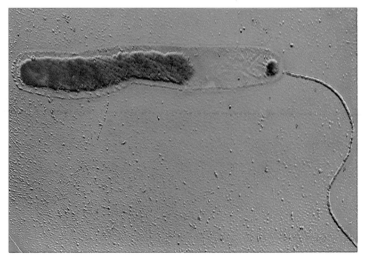

CHILD LABOUR

About 100 million children around the world are forced to work. Children are cheaper to employ than adults because their employers do not have to pay them as much, or make insurance and social security payments. But conditions and equipment which has been designed for adults may be dangerous for children. They tire more quickly and their lack of experience puts them in danger. Children not only risk being injured; they also miss out on school, so they cannot escape from poverty through education. Even in countries which have laws which restrict child workers, parents often let their children work to earn enough money to help feed the family.

◀ SAO PAULO

Sao Paulo is probably the fastest-growing city in the world. In 1988 there were 20 million people living there. The city has now become the most important manufacturing centre in Latin America. Yet on its outskirts it has squatter settlements where about 2 million people live. The people living in there suffer from polluted air, poor water supplies and an increasing rate of infant deaths. This shows that in many places where there is human success there is also human suffering.

Central America is made up of eight countries, and is home to 130 million people. The Caribbean islands lie in an arc from the largest, Cuba, to one of the smallest, Grenada. The population of the region is mixed. There are many native Indians, Europeans and descendants of African slaves, brought over to work in the plantations, where they grew crops such as sugar cane. Today, throughout the region, there is a great contrast between rich and poor people.

▲ MEXICO CITY

Between 1940 and 1970 the population of Mexico trebled. Today there are more than 90 million people, 20 million of whom live in Mexico City. The city is particularly important to the country as nearly half of its wealth is produced there. One thousand new people arrive each day. They swell the shanty towns which have grown up around the main city. Smog levels in 1988 were higher than the levels laid down by the World Health Organisation on 312 days of the year.

In January 1989 the smog was so bad that schoolchildren were given the whole month off. The smog is caused by the exhaust fumes of 2.5 million vehicles and 130,000 factories. Breathing air like this has the same effect as smoking about 40 cigarettes a day. The closeness of factories and people's homes, especially in slum areas, means that when industrial accidents happen many people suffer. When a petroleum plant exploded in the San Juanico area of Mexico City, more than 450 people were killed, 4,000 injured and 30,000 made homeless.

▼ LACANDON

The Lacandon live in the state of Chiapas on the Mexican and Guatemalan borders. There are only about 300 members of this tribe left. They have a **subsistence** form of agriculture in the rain forests of the region. They are fully protected by the Mexican government, but they are threatened by ranchers who are taking their land. The Lacandon people are the purest descendants of the Maya. The Maya were a once great civilisation based in Mexico, who built immense temple cities of stone.

WAR

Since 1970 there has been civil war in Guatemala, El Salvador, Nicaragua and Haiti. There have also been disputes over country boundaries between El Salvador and Honduras, Belize and Guatemala, Honduras and Nicaragua, and Nicaragua and Costa Rica. Many of these are due to land ownership. For example, in Guatemala two per cent of the population owns 60 per cent of the farmland. In El Salvador, until relatively recently, just 14 families owned most of the land.

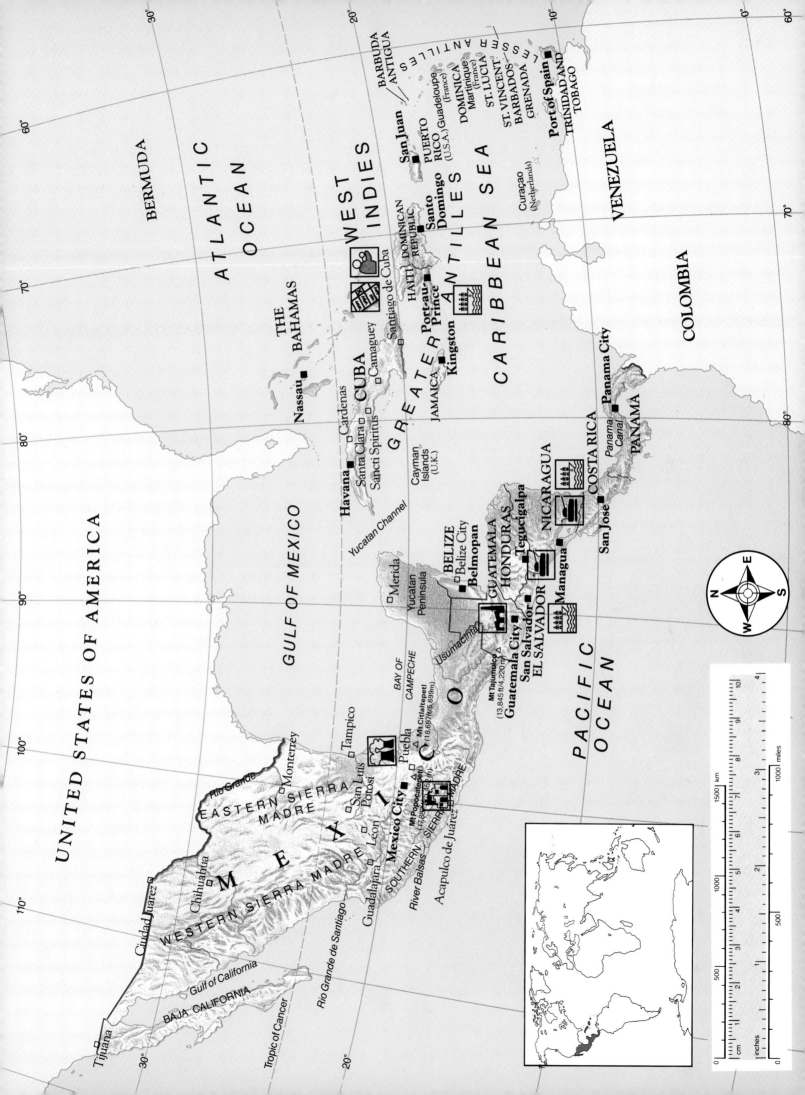

UNITED STATES OF AMERICA

The USA is a vast and rich country, with 50 states which are full of geographical variety and contrast. Its first inhabitants arrived from Siberia, crossing land which is now below the Bering Sea. They slowly spread across the whole continent.

When Europeans arrived in the sixteenth century, there were more than a million native Americans. Today, the USA is the most powerful country on Earth, with a population of over 240 million; but it has its share of problems.

▼ SEX-CHANGE POLLUTION

Research in Florida swamps has shown that the males of many animals including alligators, lizards and fish, are showing signs of becoming more female. Scientists suspect that chemicals in the environment are causing these changes. Many chemicals found in detergents, such as washing-up liquid, have a similar effect to natural chemicals called oestrogens. These are hormones and play a part in determining the sex of an animal. Some scientists think that these same chemicals, which are used all over the developed world, are changing the development of young boys and may be increasing their chances of getting cancer.

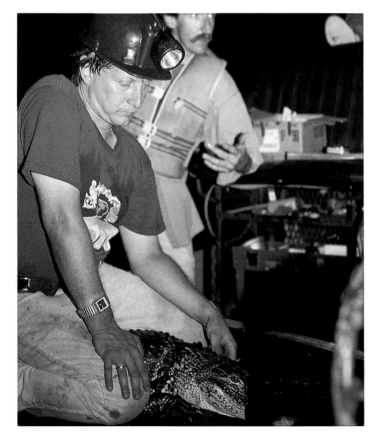

▲ AIDS

This is a relatively recent but very deadly virus that stops the body from fighting off infections and diseases. The virus can change, so it is very difficult to treat. People with the virus are known as HIV positive and often live for several years before developing full AIDS (Acquired Immune Deficiency Syndrome). Some people have been able to avoid the full effects of the virus by changing their way of life. They change the food they eat and the places they go to. This is easier to do in the USA because the quality of life and the health care standards there are very high. In regions such as Africa, AIDS is difficult to keep at bay because basic facilities such as clean water are not available to everyone. Many sufferers cannot afford health care. The conditions in many developing countries make it more difficult for people with AIDS to survive and many more people are dying of the disease in African countries than in the USA.

▼ SMOG

Los Angeles is a city in California with a geographical setting that creates problems. The city lies in a basin-shaped area. Fumes produced by cars and lorries react with the bright sunlight to create appalling smog. This looks like fog, but is brown in colour. It reduces visibility and can irritate people's eyes and lungs. The main pollutant is ozone which is formed when the chemicals and sunlight react together. When the ozone level is higher than 0.12 parts per million in an hour, a special warning is issued to old people. Young children may experience some difficulty in breathing. In Los Angeles this happens on average once every ten days. Although smog is a problem, there are now tighter controls on car exhaust fumes and industrial pollution. The air quality will eventually improve, and smog will be reduced.

▲ DRUGS

The developing world grows cash crops which they sell to the developed world to earn enough money to live. Very often the prices they are paid for these crops change from year to year depending on how much of each crop is grown across the world. But there is one type of crop for which there is always a market and a good price: drugs. Cocaine, marijuana and opium are grown in the developing world (see page 16) and although they are illegal, find their way to developed countries. Many have a drug problem. In some cities in the USA, drugs create violence; people who use drugs turn to crime so they can buy more drugs; their health tends to be poor and they risk catching AIDS by re-using infected needles. People and society are in danger from the effect of drugs which is in part an environmental issue.

NATURAL DISASTERS

The USA has its share of earthquakes, hurricanes and floods. A fault in the earth's crust, called the San Andreas Fault, runs the length of California. In 1994 a powerful earthquake struck Los Angeles. A few years earlier there had been one in San Francisco. The buildings in this part of America are specially constructed to withstand earthquakes, so comparatively few people died. Records show that although there are more natural disasters in the developed world, the number of lives lost is lower: 34,823 people were killed compared with almost 80,000 people in fewer disasters in the developing world.

PESTICIDES

Pesticides are chemicals that have been designed to kill living things which can damage crops or

affect people's health. Herbicides are used to destroy weeds, fungicides to control plant infections and diseases and insecticides to kill insects which threaten crops, homes and people's health. Millions of tonnes of these chemicals are used all over the world, not only on farms, but in parks, streets, offices, factories and homes. The drawback of using so many chemicals is that they can contaminate people's food, as well as the air and water. In 1962, a book called *Silent Spring* was published. It gave an early warning to the world that these chemicals could be damaging. No one is really sure what the long-term effects may be, but reports have mentioned cancers, birth defects and allergies. Since then there have been stricter controls.

UNNATURAL DISASTERS? ▶

In 1993 the River Mississippi flooded a vast area of land in the midwestern USA. People were killed, homes lost, crops ruined and livestock drowned in their thousands. A national emergency was declared. Many people believe that floods are caused by freak conditions in nature, but this is not the whole picture. The changes people make to the environment add to the problem. For example, natural **drainage patterns** around the river's delta have been altered to create farmland. This means the area is now able to absorb less water. When heavy rain falls, the rainwater runs off the land, rather than soaking deep into the earth.

SILICON VALLEY

During the early 1980s, a higher than usual number of sick children were born in a part of California. All of these children lived in a region known as Silicon Valley. During an investigation scientists discovered that chemicals in a

tank at an industrial plant were leaking into the soil. The chemicals contaminated the water supply of 16,500 homes in south San Jose. Pregnant women were particularly at risk from the effects of drinking the water. The authorities went on to test 79 factories in the region and found that 65 of them leaked poisonous

waste into the ground.
In 1985 it was estimated that 6,000 million tonnes of hazardous waste had been dumped on American soil. This still goes on today, though it happens mainly in developing countries where people have less opportunity to voice their objections and laws are less strict.

CANADA INCLUDING ALASKA

Canada is the second largest country in the world and has the longest coastline. It is home to native Indians, including the Inuit. European settlers spread across Canada from the seventeenth century and have made use of its wealth of natural resources since then. At first the settlers killed beaver, lynx, and foxes for their fur. Canada's great forests produced much of the world's timber. The Canadian prairies produce wheat that is sold all over the world. Today the region, in particular Alaska (which is part of the USA), is important as a source of oil. All these activities have affected the lives of the native peoples of this region. Their culture and lifestyle have changed enormously. Canada has a relatively small population of 25 million. Most people live in towns and cities in the southern part of the country, on the border with the USA.

▼ WASTE

All countries have a problem with waste disposal. The most difficult type of waste cannot be broken down easily. For example, in Toronto in the early 1990s, a huge dump of 14 million tyres caught fire. The toxic smoke could be seen 130 km away. People were evacuated from their homes and large amounts of oil from the dump seeped into the ground and polluted the **water table**.

▲ INUIT

There are 30,000 Inuit living in Alaska, 25,000 in Canada, 4,200 in Greenland, and 2,000 in Russia. Traditionally they lived by hunting seals, caribou, birds, whales, bears and Arctic foxes. The Inuit of Pond Island live off the east coast of Baffin Island. In the 1920s their traditions began to die out. The Hudson's Bay Trading Company encouraged them to trade their furs for items which would make their lifestyle more like that of the European settlers. By the late 1930s the Inuit were completely dependent on trade. In addition, as contact increased between white people and the Inuit, there was a growth in disease and they became more dependent on medicine. Missionaries converted many to Christianity. Today there is a great gulf between the generations as younger Inuit often follow western values and lifestyles.

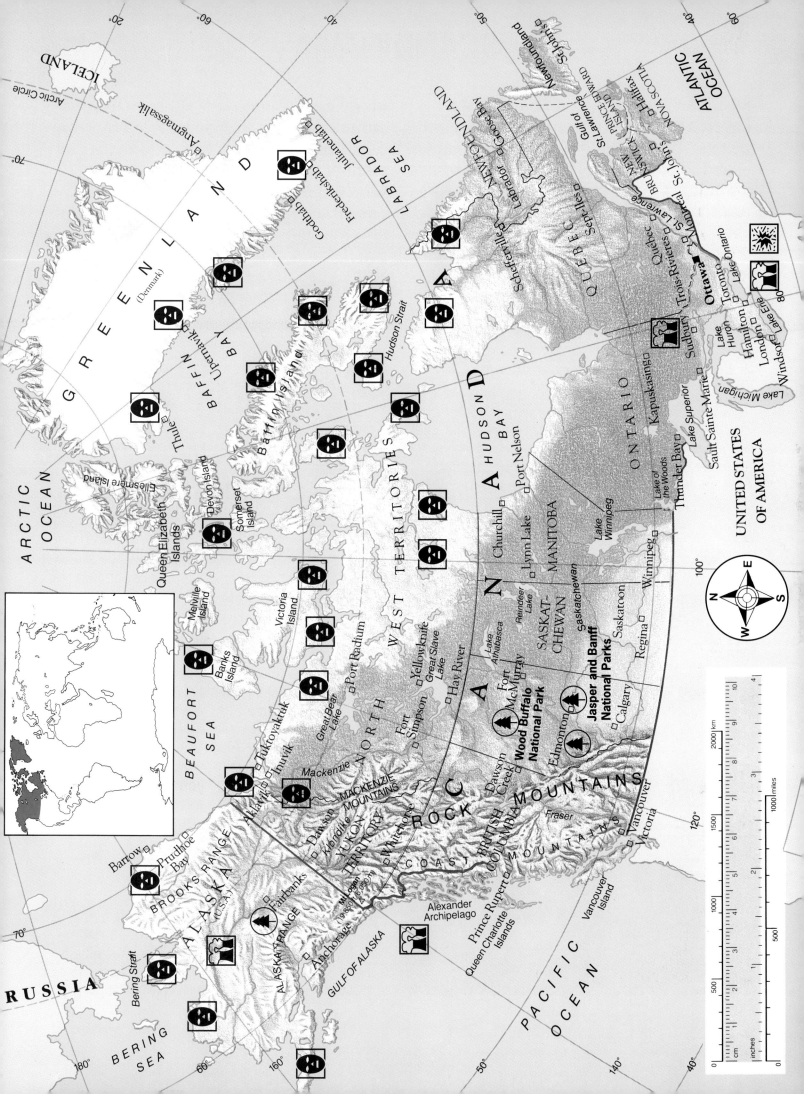

SCANDINAVIA

Five countries make up Scandinavia: Denmark, Sweden, Norway, Iceland and Finland. The total number of inhabitants is about 25 million. These countries have introduced strict laws about the way the environment should be treated and have set high standards which are followed by many other countries. Yet they have suffered from pollution created by other countries. Radiation from the damaged nuclear power station at Chernobyl affected them badly. Over a longer period the pollutants from industries in other countries have caused acid rain.

▼ SAMMI

The Sammi are the indigenous people of the Scandinavian sub-Arctic. There are 4,000 in Finland, 35,000 in Norway and 17,000 in Sweden. They originally lived a nomadic life, travelling over much larger areas than today.

The Sammi have been forced to become more settled for several reasons. Much of the land they travelled has been taken over by farmers from the south, forcing them further and further north. Their traditional migration routes have also been blocked because borders beween countries have been closed. Most of the Sammi today are settled farmers or fishermen, but some still herd reindeer in the traditional manner.

After the major nuclear accident at Chernobyl in 1986 a huge radiation cloud passed over Finland. It left both the land and the reindeer contaminated. Thousands of reindeer were slaughtered as they were not fit to be eaten. This has endangered the traditional lifestyle of these people. Today the Sammi are slowly building up their reindeer herds once again.

▲ POLLUTION WARNING

In 1988 millions of dead fish were found floating off the Scandinavian coast. They had been poisoned by algal blooms. These had multiplied because there was so much food for them in the sea. The vast numbers of **algal blooms** poisoned other life forms, such as fish. Scientists think that the source of the extra food was nitrates used as fertilisers in **intensive farming**. So much fertiliser is put on to the soil that when it rains it is washed into rivers and lakes where it pollutes the water. It also drains through rocks into underground drinking water supplies.

Nitrate pollution has become a problem in many countries in Europe where there are high levels of nitrates in the water. Sometimes young children have been affected by water with too high nitrate levels.

Perhaps even more dangerous to people's health is the fact that pesticides are being washed into drinking water. These can be extremely dangerous to human health.

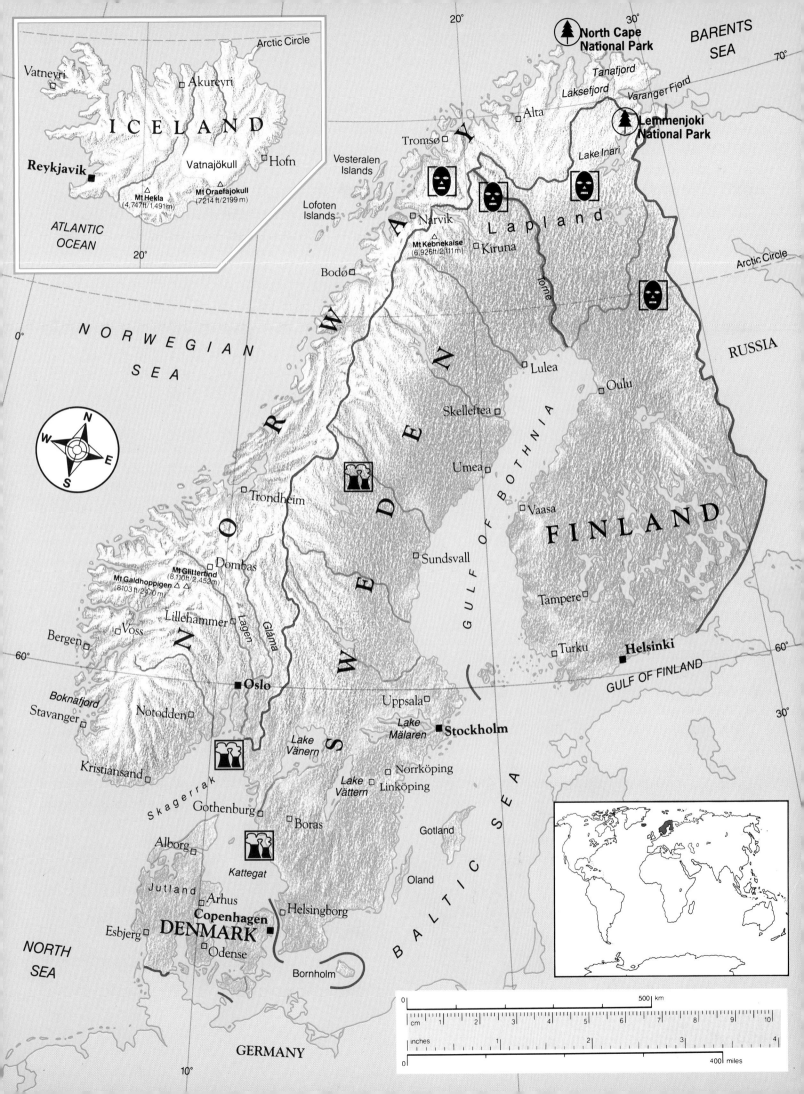

Iceland (inset)
Vatneyri
Akureyri
Arctic Circle
I C E L A N D
Vatnajökull
Hofn
Reykjavik
Mt Hekla
(4,747ft/1,491m)
Mt Oraefajokull
(7214 ft/2199 m)
ATLANTIC
OCEAN
20°

Main map
20°
30°
North Cape
National Park
BARENTS
SEA
70°
Tanafjord
Laksefjord
Varanger Fjord
Alta
Lemmenjoki
National Park
Tromsø
Lapland
Lake Inari
Vesteralen
Islands
Narvik
Mt Kebnekaise
(6,926ft/2,111m)
Kiruna
Torne
Arctic Circle
Lofoten
Islands
Bodø
RUSSIA
NORWEGIAN
SEA
0°
Lulea
N O R W E G Y
Skelleftea
Oulu
Trondheim
Umea
GULF OF BOTHNIA
FINLAND
Dombas
Vaasa
Sundsvall
Mt Glittertind
(8,110ft/2,452m)
Mt Galdhoppigen
(8103 ft/2470 m)
Tampere
Lagen
Glama
Lillehammer
Bergen
Voss
60°
Turku
Helsinki
60°
Stavanger
Notodden
Oslo
GULF OF FINLAND
Boknafjord
Uppsala
Lake
Mälaren
Stockholm
Kristiansand
S W E D E N
Skagerrak
Norrköping
Lake
Vättern
Linköping
Gothenburg
Boras
Alborg
Gotland
BALTIC SEA
Kattegat
Oland
Jutland
Arhus
Helsingborg
DENMARK
Copenhagen
Esbjerg
Odense
NORTH
SEA
Bornholm
GERMANY
10°

0   500 km
cm 1 2 3 4 5 6 7 8 9 10
inches   1   2   3   4
0   400 miles

This region of the world is where the Industrial Revolution began. The landscape has changed enormously as a result. Forests have been cut down and cities have grown up with large numbers of factories which have polluted the air. There has also been great social change in the last 100 years. Many people moved from the country to live and work in cities. This is now happening in many parts of the developing world today. This part of Europe is relatively crowded. There are about 300 million people living in the 14 countries.

▲ ASTHMA ATTACKS

Asthma attacks are increasing in many western European cities. The main cause for this is not clear, but an increase in pollution from car fumes may take some of the blame. Sunlight converts the chemicals in exhaust fumes into ozone, which is damaging when breathed in. Paris and Madrid are considered to have unacceptable levels of pollution in their air and London's air quality is marginal. The German city of Frankfurt, on the other hand, has cleaner air.

MODERN DISEASES

Most people living in the developed world have clean water, good general healthcare and vaccinations to protect them from diseases. This makes them healthier than many of the people living in developing countries. But it does not mean they are disease-free. Health statistics show that a typical European lifestyle can lead to heart disease and some forms of cancer. These may partly be caused by a combination of a rich diet and too little exercise.

▼ CHEMICAL ACCIDENTS

On 10 July 1976 an explosion at a chemical factory in the north Italian town of Seveso released a cloud of the deadly chemical dioxin into the atmosphere. No one died, but 200 people were badly injured and 1,800 hectares of the land around the region was contaminated. Many animals were killed (see below). No one was allowed to go near the land for over six years.

On 1 November 1986 a fire broke out at a warehouse near Basle in Switzerland. The warehouse contained about 1,300 tonnes of 90 different chemicals. As the warehouse burned, the chemicals polluted the atmosphere, and the water of the River Rhine. They also poisoned the soil and drained into the ground water. No one was killed, but the ground water in the underground rocks around the Rhine is still polluted. This may affect the quality of people's drinking water for many years to come.

60° 10° Faeroe
Islands
(Denmark) 0° 10° 20° FINLAND
60°
Shetland
Islands NORWAY
60°
Orkney
Islands

Ben Nevis
(4,406 ft / 1,343 m)
△
SCOTLAND
Glasgow □ Edinburgh
UNITED
NORTHERN
IRELAND □ Belfast ③
KINGDOM
Galway
IRELAND ■ Dublin
IRISH
SEA Liverpool Manchester ②
Cork WALES

DENMARK
NORTH
SEA
Kiel □ Rostock
Hamburg
Elbe
Hanover Berlin
POLAND
Oder
Leipzig
Weimar Dresden
Jena

1 Snowdonia
National Park

2 Peak District
National Park

3 Lake District
National Park

50°
NETHERLANDS
Amsterdam
Utrecht
Ijsselmeer
The Hague
Dover Maastricht
Bruges Cologne
Calais Brussels
Lille Liège Bonn
BELGIUM Frankfurt
Main
Mannheim
LUXEMBOURG
Luxembourg
GERMANY
Bavarian Forest
National Park
CZECH REPUBLIC
SLOVAKIA

London
Plymouth
ENGLISH CHANNEL
Channel
Islands
(U.K.)
50°

ATLANTIC
OCEAN
Paris
Strasbourg
Rhine Munich
Salzburg
Vienna
AUSTRIA
Graz
HUNGARY
20°

Nantes
Dijon
FRANCE
Vosges
Basle
Zurich
Innsbruck
LIECHTENSTEIN SLOVENIA
Mt Grossglockner
(12,467 ft / 3,797 m)
Berne
SWITZERLAND
Trieste
CROATIA

BAY OF BISCAY
CENTRAL
MASSIF
Lyon
Lausanne
Mont Blanc
(15,771 ft / 4,807 m) △
Milan
Verona
Venice
SANMARINO
ADRIATIC SEA

Bordeaux
Dordogne
Garonne
Po
Turin
Bologna

Rhône
Avignon
MONACO
Genoa
Florence
APENNINES
Rome
Abruzzo
National Park
Bari

CANTABRIAN MOUNTAINS
Bilbao
Toulouse
Marseille
Camargue
Regional Park
Corsica
(France)
ITALY

10°
Porto
Pico de Aneto
(11,168 ft / 3,404 m)
PYRENEES
ANDORRA

Duero
Zaragoza
Ebro
Naples
10°

Málaga
Mt Mulhacén
(11,411 ft / 3,478 m) △

Coto Donana
Reserve

Gibraltar
(United Kingdom)

MOROCCO

PORTUGAL
Tagus
SPAIN
Madrid
Lisbon
Guadiana
Córdoba
Seville Guadalquivir

Barcelona
40°
Majorca
Valencia
Balearic Islands

Sardinia

Palermo
Marsala
Sicily
Messina
Catania

MEDITERRANEAN SEA

N
W E
S

ALGERIA
TUNISIA
Valletta
MALTA

500 1000 km
cm 1 2 3 4 5 6 7 8 9 10
inches 1 2 3 4
0 500 miles

EAST EUROPE

The recent history of the countries in this region has been influenced by communism. People have either a traditional, rural way of life in the country, or a very industrialised one in the cities. Albania is the exception to this. It has been very cut off from the rest of the world and most of its people live in the country. In many countries different ethnic groups live together. This has led to civil war in former Yugoslavia and tension in other countries in this region.

CIVIL WAR ▶

Civil war has raged in the former Yugoslavia since 1992. Thousands of people have died and many cities, towns and villages have been bombed and destroyed. Yugoslavia no longer exists and people from the different ethnic groups (Serbs, Croats, Christians and Muslims) will never live together in the same way as before. Single communities were once mixed, but they have been torn apart and the bitterness left may never heal. All sides seem to have committed atrocities and to be guilty of land-grabbing.

▼ POLLUTION

The pollution in this region has never been successfully controlled. This has happened in many industrialised parts of the world which were previously under communist rule. As a result many of the people who live and work in the cities are at risk from diseases associated with pollution. In Hungary one death in 17 is thought to be caused by pollution. Northern Poland has one of the highest rates of nitrates in its rain and snow. An area over Poland, former Czechoslovakia and the Russian border has very high levels of ammonia in its rainwater. In many countries, lead in petrol can cause health problems. If too much lead is absorbed by the human body, it affects the development of the brain, especially in babies and young children. This can be reduced if cars use lead-free petrol, but not all countries have adopted this policy yet.

CHANGE

Nearly all the countries in this region were communist and had close economic links with the USSR. People have been finding new ways of life since the break-up of the USSR and the end of communist rule in many countries.

The future is made all the more uncertain because of the complicated history of the region. During the two world wars this century, world powers such as the USA, Britain and France have intervened in creating country boundaries. Czechoslovakia was formed in 1919, throwing together Czechs and Slovaks. Nowadays there is more awareness of the differences between ethnic groups, held unhappily together by country boundaries. The future is very uncertain and events such as the civil war in Yugoslavia are not encouraging.

NORTHERN AFRICA

This region has some of the world's harshest landscapes and poorest countries. It is dominated by the Sahara desert. A temperature of 58˚C was recorded in Libya in 1922 and this remains the hottest on record. Many peoples have lived here for thousands of years, making the most of what the land offers. War, drought and growing deserts add to the problems many people face.

REFUGEES ▼

The United Nations defines a refugee as a person who cannot return to his or her own country because of a 'well-founded fear of persecution for reasons of race, religion, nationality, political association or grouping'. But there are also environmental refugees.

These are people who have been driven from their homes because they can no longer live off the land. These people do not always have help from other countries in the world. During the early 1980s in Africa at least 10 million people were forced into refugee camps or into city slums because they could no longer grow food on their infertile land.

WAR ▲

Many of the countries in this region, such as Sudan, Chad, Ethiopia and Somalia are suffering from war. Some people believe that it is war, and not drought, that has led to the starvation of millions of people in the region. In Ethiopia at one point half the country's money was spent on weapons.

This put an enormous strain on the already fragile economy. The government put pressure on farmers to grow extra cash crops, which resulted in there being fewer food crops available.

Even during the years of drought, food products have been exported in increasing numbers. It is war rather than drought which puts people in danger from starvation.

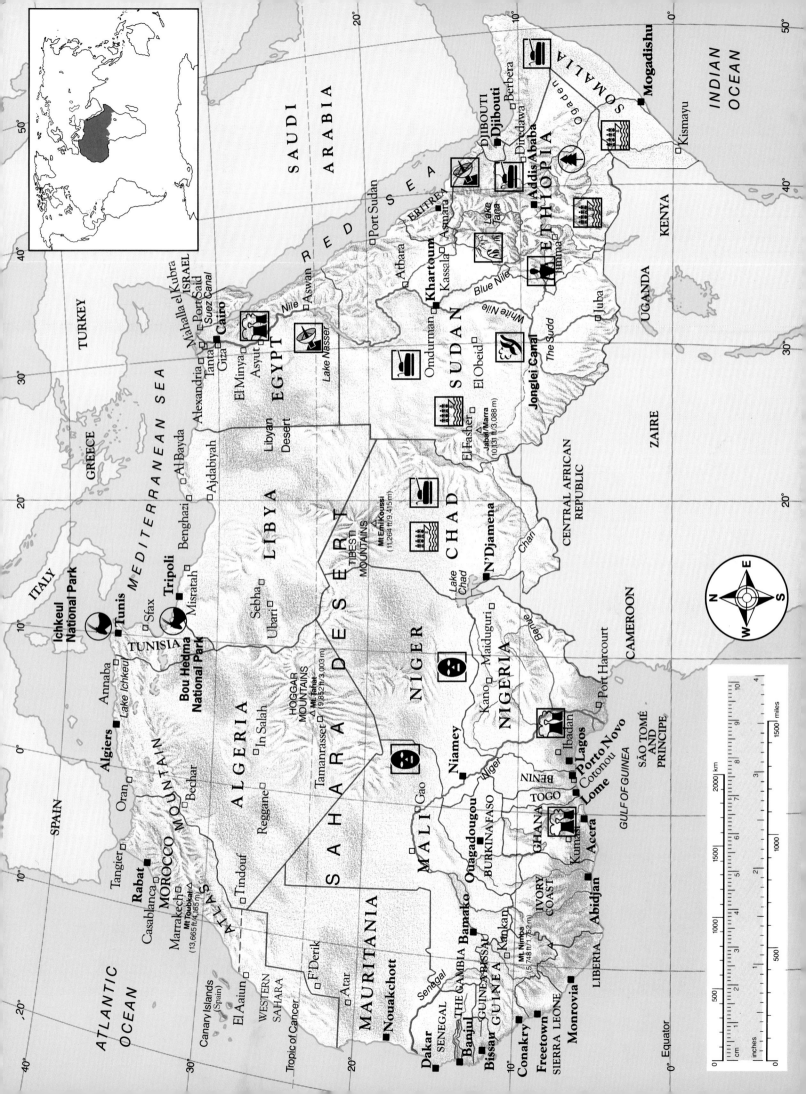

▼ THE TUAREG

The Tuareg's way of life has changed dramatically in the last 20 years. They were originally nomads, depending on herds of sheep, camels and goats for their needs. They would travel more than 1,500 km across the Sahara desert to trade in salt, animals and animal produce. They also owned gardens tended by the Harratin, people who were descended from African slaves. Today the Harratin own the gardens and trade their crops for the animal products of the Tuareg.

The constant threat of drought has meant that it is increasingly difficult for the Tuareg to be as nomadic as they used to be. Modern governments prefer their people to be more settled than the Tuareg like to be. These pressures have a slowly eroding effect on their traditional lifestyle.

LIVING ON PEANUTS

In the 1950s and 1960s, growing peanuts became an increasingly important way for people to earn money. But to grow peanuts year after year, the soil needs to be regularly fertilised. Most peasant farmers were unable to afford the fertilisers.

The land was originally grazed by the animals of visiting nomadic tribes who would trade with the peasant farmers. These animals would leave their dung which would fertilise the soil. But the peanut crops forced the nomads to graze their animals elsewhere, on land which eventually turned into desert.

The result has been that the crops of peanuts have become smaller and more land has been turned into desert. In the Sudan, for example, one hectare of land in 1961 produced the same amount of peanuts as five hectares in 1973.

◀ THE ASWAN HIGH DAM

In Egypt, there is less water than people need to grow crops and for industry. In addition, the water supply is never very reliable. So the Aswan Dam was built across the River Nile which created a huge new reservoir called Lake Nasser.

More than 40,000 people had to be moved before the dam could be built. Although it now provides half of Egypt's electricity and has reduced flood damage, it has created problems.

Before the dam was built, the waters of the Nile would flood, leaving mud and silt on the land. This was a natural fertiliser. Now the silt is being trapped in Lake Nasser. Scientists think that in about 100 years time the lake will be completely filled with silt. Also, farmers have to buy artificial fertilisers today, rather than have the free silt provided by the Nile.

The dam has helped to water crops. But many of the channels built to carry the water hold animals such as water snails which carry the fatal disease bilharzia (see page 46). Large dam building projects all over the world have created as many problems as they solve.

LOCUST PLAGUES

Locusts are a type of grasshopper which swarm in alarming numbers when the conditions are right. A swarm may cover 1,000 square kilometres and contain as many as 40,000 million locusts. This number could eat as much food in one day as 400,000 people could eat in one year!

The locusts start their life hatching from eggs laid in the sand. They quickly develop wings and become airborne. It is at this stage that they are dangerous and difficult to control. They will land on any vegetation and eat it all in a matter of hours. Vital food crops can be completely ruined and people face total starvation after a swarm has landed. In Ethiopia in 1958, locusts ate 150,000 tonnes of cereals – about the amount needed to feed a million people for a year. Today, satellites watch out for hatching swarms, which can then be killed with chemicals.

DROUGHT AND DESERTS ▼

During the 1980s, severe droughts caused problems in many parts of Africa. But the droughts often affected quite small areas. Problems arose when people tried to produce more crops. In addition there was over-grazing by goats, sheep and cattle, and people cut down trees for fuel. All these factors led to growing deserts. In Ethiopia, the forests in the highlands once held the fertile soil in place. Now every year about a billion metric tonnes of **topsoil** is washed away because the trees have been cut down and the soil eroded by wind and rain. In the next 25 years Ethiopia will lose 100,000 hectares of topsoil from its land.

CENTRAL AND SOUTHERN AFRICA

Scientists think that this part of Africa is where the first humans lived. Humans soon spread to other parts of the world and 1.8 million years later have become the most dominant species on Earth. Today this part of Africa is a varied region, where traditional and colonial influences are mixed. Countries have the typical problems of rural communities and large and growing cities. Migration adds to the pressure on urban life. The largest city is Kinshasa, capital of Zaire, with more than 3 million people. The area's population is about 200 million.

MONEY WITH TIES

Developing countries are often offered advice, expertise and equipment from countries which are more technologically advanced. But this rarely comes without a catch. For example, the Tanzanian government were offered expensive combine harvesters, seed and know-how from well-trained experts on improving wheatcrops. They accepted the help, but had to agree that in future Tanzania would buy all its materials and equipment from Canada. Now, when new fertiliser or spare parts for the combine harvesters are needed, neither the farmers nor the government can afford to buy them. So the combine harvesters have been left to rust and the wheat fields are unharvested. This is an example of an arrangement between two countries that benefited neither.

▲ THE BAKA PYGMIES

The Baka are a tribe of pygmies who live in south-east Cameroon and the northern forests of the Congo. They have remained isolated from the Bantu, the other people who live in the region, until recently. Traditionally, they have hunted with spears and dogs and collected wild honey. Their way of life is threatened, both through rain forest destruction and trading with the Bantu, from whom they get supplies. In recent years they have become more and more dependent on the powerful Bantu.

▼ SOUTH AFRICA

The recent history of South Africa has been dominated by **apartheid**. The struggle for equality for all people in South Africa has been a long one, but there have been significant moves towards full democracy in the early 1990s.

The control that the white minority has had over political and economic power is finally being loosened. The first full elections the country has known were held in April 1994. But change of this sort can be dangerous. Rival groups who want to bring about change have argued and fought, and people have been killed.

SOUTH-WEST ASIA

This region has been scarred by war between rival groups fighting for territory, resources such as oil, or the right to govern in a particular way and follow a particular religion. Many people have died in the past 30 years especially when Iran and Iraq were at war (1980–1989).

The Iraqi invasion of Kuwait in 1991 caused a major international incident involving the United Nations. Israel has been in constant conflict with neighbouring Arab nations and there has been civil war in Lebanon between different religious groups.

KURDS

The Kurds are a Muslim people who have no country of their own. They are spread between Turkey, Iran, Iraq, Syria and some previously Soviet states. The Kurds are the world's largest stateless minority, with a population of more than 16 million.

They are persecuted in many places. For example, in 1988 the government in Iraq used chemical weapons to kill thousands of Kurdish villagers. Many fled across the Turkish border to escape.

After Iraq's invasion of Kuwait, the plight of the Kurds became an international issue and they were protected by soldiers from the United Nations. Their suffering continues today, although they have continually sought international help. Their aim is to set up an independent state, called Kurdistan.

▲ MARSH ARABS

In southern Iraq, where the delta of the River Euphrates makes a vast fertile marsh, live the Marsh Arabs. They have changed very little over thousands of years, fishing and using the natural resources of the delta. They build their boats and houses from reeds.

The Iraqi government sees these people as a threat and has poisoned the river water and bombed and drained the marshes. Their unique way of life is under attack and so is their environment.

▼ MALARIA

Malaria is a threat to people living in this part of the world, although there are fewer cases than there once were. Malaria is a disease spread by the bite of a species of mosquito.

The symptoms are caused by a microscopic single-celled organism which lives in the blood.

In 1988, 8 million cases were reported worldwide to the World Health Organisation, but the real number of cases is more like 100 million. Just under half of the world's people live in areas where malaria occurs. Malaria is found in 102 countries but since 1980 there has been a general decrease in Africa, South-East Asia, and the Western Pacific, but a gradual increase in Central and South America. It can be controlled by treating people with drugs and by draining areas of stagnant water.

RUSSIA AND ITS NEIGHBOURS

Russia and its neighbours make up the former USSR. This is an extremely complex region, with more than 300 million people, who speak more than 60 languages. Since the USSR has broken up, the many ethnic groups within the new countries formed have all made claims to power. Political change has brought widespread social and economic difficulties. People living in the region suffer from both high unemployment and inflation.

THE NENTSI ▶

There are two distinct groups of these traditional peoples in Russia. One is the tundra Nentsi, whose way of life depends on hunting sea mammals, but who also herd reindeer like the Sammi (see page 26). The other is the forest Nentsi, a much smaller group who live by fishing in rivers for salmon and sturgeon and by farming the land.

After the 1930s, the Russians moved the Nentsi on to farmland. They had to live in large, settled villages. Changes in their way of life were forced upon them. For example, when the adults went hunting, the children had to stay in schools. The Nentsi fear that their skills passed down from generation to generation will disappear altogether. When indigenous peoples are made to fit in with other peoples' cultures, their own very quickly become lost.

POLLUTION

Pollution is a serious threat in Russia. It is particularly bad in Siberia. Although it is a freezing wasteland in winter, Siberia is heavily exploited. There are mines extracting minerals, from coal to valuable metal ores. There are oil pipelines and large **hydroelectric** schemes. It has been very well developed, but some of the industries have been allowed to run down. There has been very little environmental control. For example, the oil pipelines are now old and leak. Industries have grown up around large lakes such as

Baikal, which have become heavily polluted. Indigenous people, who rely on natural resources, are particularly badly affected. Polluted water and poisoned fish limit their ability to carry on with their way of life. In the long term all people, whether indigenous or otherwise, are placed in danger from such pollution.

NUCLEAR DISASTER ▼

1986 was a turning point for the future safety of people all over the world. On 26 April a huge explosion took place at the nuclear power station in Chernobyl. It released so much radioactivity into the environment that 31 people died. Between 20,000 and 40,000 people are expected to die of cancer in the CIS (Commonwealth of Independent states) and Europe during the next 30 to 60 years. It is the long-term, unknown effects of nuclear power which put people at risk.

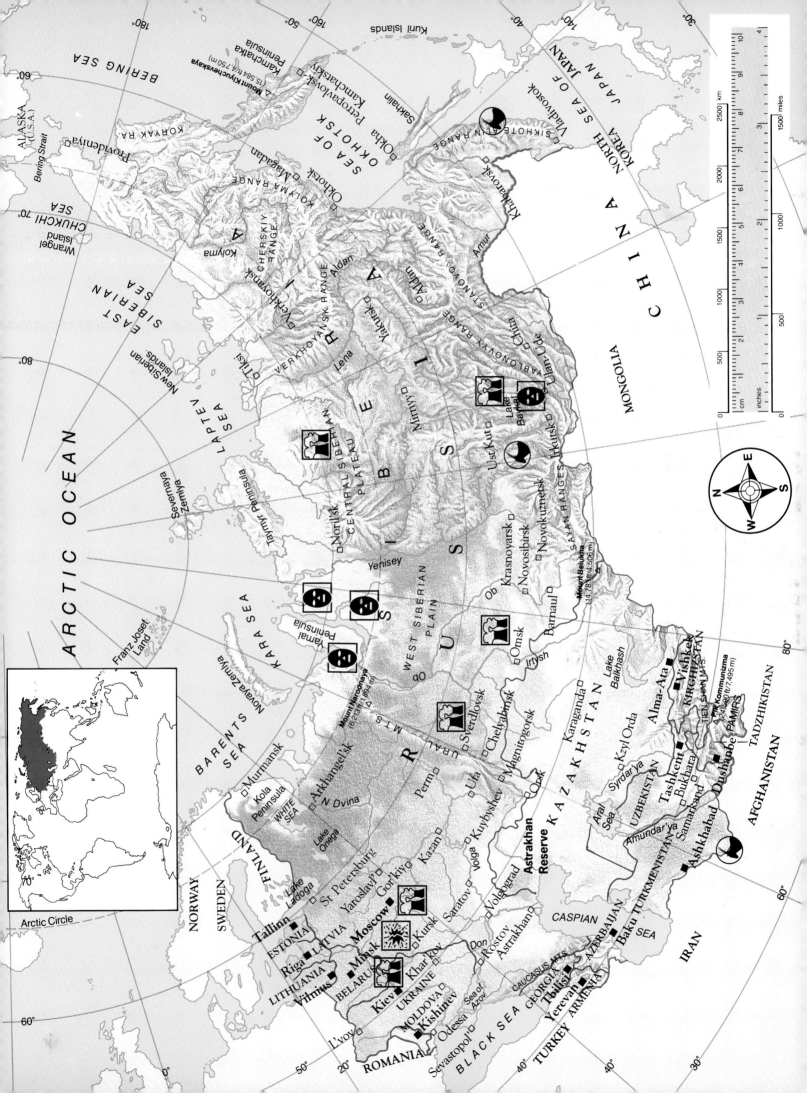

INDIA AND ITS NEIGHBOURS

More than 1,000 million people live in the eight countries in this region. India, Pakistan and Bangladesh have many severely overcrowded cities. Calcutta alone has a population of more than 10 million. There have always been problems between different religious groups in the region (especially between Muslims and Hindus). Cutting down the forests in the foothills of the Himalayas has caused many environmental problems which threaten human life. In addition, war is a constant threat and borders are jealously guarded.

▲ PEOPLE VERSUS NATURE

All over the world national parks have been created to help conserve wildlife. This may be for tourism (which brings in valuable foreign money) or it may be to save a particular species from extinction. But national parks are not always good for the people who live in them. These people can lose some of their freedom and may even be forced to move. Where once the people of the region could hunt for meat, they become poachers. In the Sunderbans National Park, people are at risk from tigers, which the park was created to save. About 30 to 50 people are killed each year by the tigers that live in the park. People do not enter the park, but a number of tigers hunt outside the park's boundaries. The tigers are protected, so the local people cannot do anything about it. This causes tension between the local people and the park administrators.

▼ BHOPAL

In the city of Bhopal on the night of 2 December 1984 there was a

sudden and unexpected release of about 30 tonnes of a poisonous gas, methyl isocyanate, from a pesticide factory. The gas was heavier than air and formed a blanket on the ground. This spread through the city and the surrounding shanty towns. Nearly 2,800 people died as a result of breathing the poisonous gas. Another 20,000 experienced breathing difficulties and damage to their lungs and eyes.

Even today people in the city suffer from the after effects of the accident. It was caused by poor safety procedures. The effects were made worse by the fact that the company had chosen to build its factory close to an area where hundreds of people lived. This would not have been allowed in developed countries. Accidents of this sort are worse in the developing world because so many people live in shanty towns built on land which no one else wants.

▲ BANGLADESH

Bangladesh has the largest delta in the world. It is flat except for a few hills in the north and the south-east. The land is fertile but floods easily. During floods many people die and their homes are washed away. In April 1991 a cyclone caused the death of about 125,000 people.

The floods in Bangladesh also have an effect on the soil. Iodine, which is an essential chemical for human health, is washed out of the soil into the sea. About 20 million people beome ill because of a lack of iodine in their diet. Lack of iodine can cause mental illness and may prevent normal development and growth. A swelling of the thyroid gland in the throat, known as a goitre, is the most obvious symptom. Children born to mothers who do not have enough iodine may have physical and mental problems which can never be cured. This could be avoided by giving people a small, regular supply of iodine in their diet. The Bangladeshi government now puts iodine in salt, but not everyone is willing to pay for this. Many are slow to accept a change in the taste or appearance of their food. The health of the people and the success of the country are both affected as a direct result of the environmental conditions in which people live.

▼ NARMADA VALLEY

In the Narmada Valley an ambitious scheme to build 3,000 dams across the Narmada River caused many problems. The local people, including members of the Bhils and Tadavis tribes, will lose land and homes if the project goes ahead. If the Sardar Sarovar dam (the largest planned) is built, 250 villages will be submerged. More than 100,000 local people, including 60,000 tribespeople, will have to leave their homes.

Some people thought that the dams were necessary to help deal with droughts. But the people who planned the dams planned to pipe any water left over after watering the crops to cities rather than to rural areas.

Some people argued that the money would be better spent on small-scale local projects, such as wells, water pumps and small dams. These would cost less and benefit local people. No one would have to move from their homes, and there would be less damage to the environment.

After a campaign involving an international organisation, the countries supplying the money to pay for the dams changed their minds. The Bhils and Tadavis can continue their lives farming, hunting and fishing, for the time being.

LANDSLIDES IN SRI LANKA

In 1989 the Kegalle region in Sri Lanka was struck by landslides which killed 171 people and forced 25,000 to leave their homes. An entire village was buried in mud. The landslides in the region were set off by the heavy **monsoon** rains. Rainfall of more than 40 cm fell in one area and some parts of the region were flooded under 10 metres of water. This is not unusual in some parts of the world. But heavy rain can be deadly in hilly areas where the trees and other vegetation have been cut down. In these conditions, the soil is likely to be washed down the slopes by torrential rain and set off a landslide.

▲ THE GONDS

This group is the largest of all the tribal peoples in India. The Gonds live in the forested areas between the Vindhya mountains and the Eastern Ghats. They practise shifting cultivation, moving through the forests. But increasing population levels, invasion of the land by outsiders, forestry and mining projects as well as dam building, have forced them to become more settled in their living and agricultural ways.

THE VEDDAS

Sri Lanka was invaded in 500 BC and the local inhabitants were driven into the interior. Today, about 2,000 of the Veddas' descendants survive, but only a few hundred continue the hunter-gatherer way of life of their ancestors. Their traditional lifestyle is now threatened by the creation of a national park. The park will protect the forests and attract foreign money, but will end a way of life that has existed for thousands of years.

▼ TROUBLED TIMES

There has been a lot of violence in this region as different groups fight over land and seek independence from those who do not share the same religious faiths or views. Today this violence continues in different countries as people try to form new states which are independent of the main nation.

Afghanistan was occupied by the Soviets in 1979. They were forced to leave in 1989. The victorious groups who removed the Soviets from their country are now fighting each other for control. Millions of people have been killed or forced to flee as refugees as a result.

Sri Lanka is an island with a total population of 20 million, of which nearly 3.5 million make up a minority group called the Tamils. The Tamils want to form an independent state in the north of the country. Constant fighting between the Tamils and the Sri Lankan army has caused the deaths of thousands of people.

The people of Bangladesh fought for independence from Pakistan. This led to civil war and eventually to independence in 1971. The fighting between East Pakistan, as Bangladesh was called, and the military forces of West Pakistan, as it was then known, caused the deaths of a million people and forced another 8 million to flee to India to escape from attack.

CHINA, JAPAN AND THEIR NEIGHBOURS

In this region of great contrasts is the country with the largest population on Earth: China. There are more than 1,250 million Chinese people. The country is communist and most people live in rural areas. It also has a few enormous cities, including Beijing, the capital. Rice is people's main food. Famine has been a major threat to life, killing many thousands when it struck. Japan is an advanced industrial nation. People enjoy a high standard of living. But pollution and overcrowding are a threat to this. Japan lies on a major geological fault line, which means it suffers from severe earthquakes.

CONTROLLING THE POPULATION

China has a severe population problem. The country can feed no more than 1,200 million people. By the early 1980s there were already well over 1,000 million Chinese.

As a result, the government brought in a policy that allows families to have only one child. This may suit some people who live in crowded cities, but in rural communities people tend to have large families. The family members help to tend the crops and look after the animals.

In China today there are now many spoilt only children. Chinese parents tend to prefer boys and there have been several scandals which have involved the murder of baby girls. Solving China's population problem seems likely to take a long time.

◄ BILHARZIA

Human beings have always died from diseases. But the way people live or the way they change the natural environment can make all the difference to whether a disease can be kept in check. For example, a disease called bilharzia (or schistosomiasis), which causes dysentery and anaemia, is caused by a **blood fluke** which lives for part of its life in a water snail. The water snail thrives in places where rice is grown.

Rice is cultivated in huge areas of China. Fields are flooded and farmers plant the rice seedlings. The young of the blood fluke leave the snails and burrow through human skin to reach people's blood stream. Around the world today about 200 million people are infected with bilharzia and 600 million more are at risk from it.

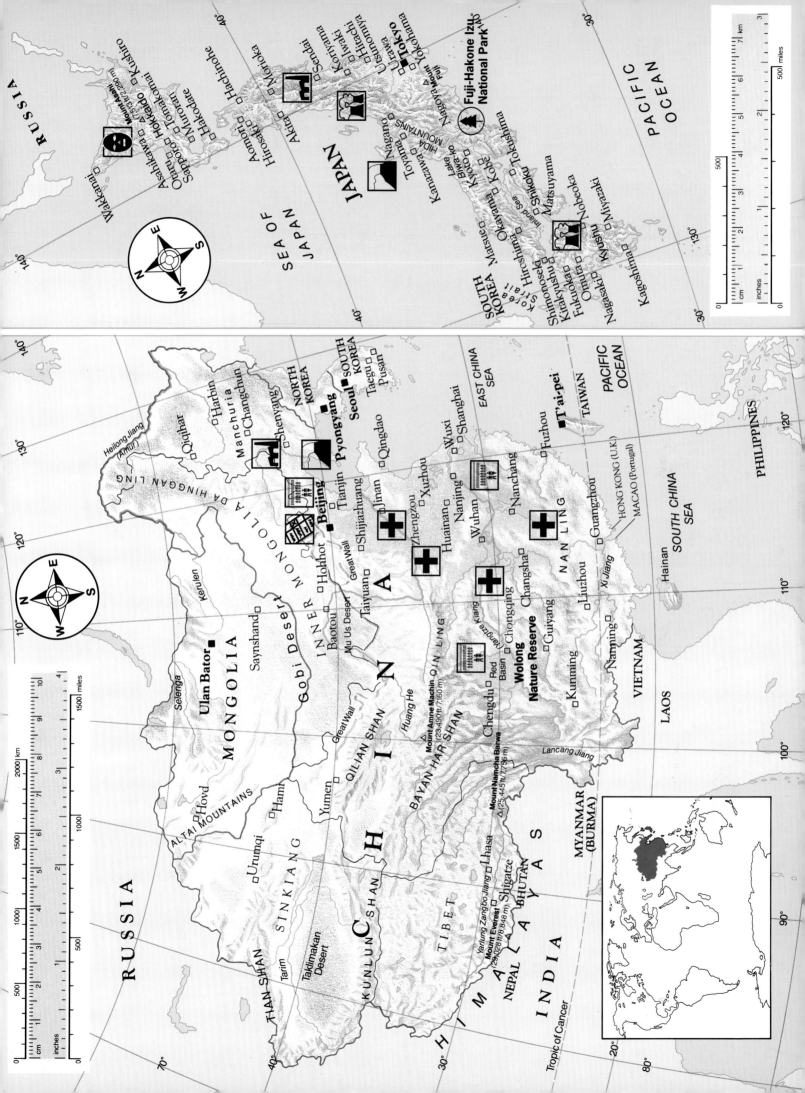

In the 1960s, China's communist leader, Chairman Mao, decided that people should spend much of their time collecting scraps of steel. This was intended to help China move towards industrialisation. Even farmers were encouraged to do this rather than to work in their fields and grow food crops.

As a result many people died of starvation. During the decade millions of people died because not enough food was being grown. This was despite the fact that there is enough land in China to feed the whole nation.

MERCURY POISONING

Minamata is a town on the Japanese island of Kyushu. In the late 1950s, a factory there pumped methylmercury, a poisonous chemical, into the sea. This contaminated the fish and other marine animals, which in turn poisoned the people who ate them.

As a result of this, and a similar incident at Niigata on the east coast of Honshu, 400 Japanese people died, Another 2,000 people suffered from the effects of the poison. This is an extreme example of the dangers to human life from dumping chemical wastes in the sea.

CITY POLLUTION

Chinese people who live in cities are much more likely to die of lung cancer than the people who live in rural areas. This is because the amount of sulphur dioxide in the air is four times higher than the recommended acceptable level (set by the World Health Organisation) in the centre of the Chinese capital Beijing. Sulphur dioxide is the chemical which causes acid rain.

Another Chinese city called Benxi, on the borders of North Korea, is China's (and possibly the world's) most polluted city. Here, half of the 420 factories contribute to the air pollution which each year totals 213,000 metric tonnes of smoke and dust and 87 million cubic metres of polluting gases. People who live there are six times more likely than other people to suffer from serious diseases.

INDUSTRIALISATION

Many developing countries want to be able to produce goods and sell them for a profit elsewhere in the world. Japan and Hong Kong are good examples of industrialised countries in this part of the world. Both countries trade with many others in the world. Japan sells goods, and Hong Kong sells mainly services, such as banking. China, which has a huge population and considerable natural resources, wants to become more industrialised. Although the process need not put people in danger, careful planning and preparation are needed to avoid the problems which developing countries all over the world are going through. These include pollution from factories, the build up of shanty towns around industrial areas, migration from rural areas and the lower quality of facilities such as water. These are only avoided if the country can ensure that changes happen in a controlled way. There are 12 million people living in Tokyo and another 20 million live around the city. In Hong Kong nearly 6 million people are squeezed into a tiny area. Both these cities are rich and can therefore plan well. China's cities are far poorer and so they face far greater problems.

▲ EARTHQUAKES

This part of the world is under threat from earthquakes and volcanic activity. The last major earthquake to hit Tokyo and Yokohama happened in 1923. The earthquake was known as the Great Kanto quake and it destroyed 370,000 buildings, killed 59,000 people and made another 2.5 million people homeless. Today, the buildings in Japanese cities are designed and built to withstand earthquakes. Special equipment is used to predict when earthquakes are likely to happen in all parts of this region. People are trained to know what to do should an earthquake strike. In China in July 1966, an unpredicted earthquake hit the city of Tangshan and destroyed it in seconds, killing 240,000 people. Even with elaborate and expensive equipment it is not always possible to avoid the danger from natural disasters.

INDIGENOUS PEOPLE ▼

The Ainu are the original inhabitants of the Japanese islands. These people have their own language and cultural traditions but they have been slowly dying out over the centuries. The present population of Ainu is around 50,000, though only a very few of them are pure blooded. They mainly live on the northern island of Hokkaido.

SOUTH-EAST ASIA

Much of South-East Asia has been torn apart by war. The Vietnam war in the 1960s killed thousands. In Cambodia, in the 1970s, more than a million people were killed by the Khmer Rouge. Land mines from the war still claim lives. One in every 236 Cambodians and one in every 1,250 Vietnamese has lost a limb from land mines. Seven out of every ten people in the Cambodian capital, Phnom Penh, used to work in the country but came to the city to find a living. Much of the region's forest is being cut down and sold. Indonesia has 13,677 islands, half of which are occupied. Indonesia has the fifth largest population in the world.

TOBACCO IN MALAYSIA

In Malaysia there are about 62,000 families involved in growing tobacco. The plants need 16 applications of insecticide before they produce a healthy crop. Some of the chemicals used in pesticides in developing countries are banned in the developed world because they are dangerous.

Tobacco leaves have to be cured or dried before they are made into cigarettes. Wood from nearby forests is burned to dry the leaves. Two to three hectares of trees are needed to cure one tonne of tobacco. About one in every eight trees felled around the world is used for this purpose. Like many cash crops, tobacco brings in a lot of money, but at a cost. About one million deaths per year are caused by cigarette smoking.

VIETNAMESE BOAT PEOPLE ▼

War and its aftermath has often led to persecution. When the Vietnam war ended in 1975, the government changed. People who had opposed the new government were now in danger. Many chose to leave. Like most refugees they had few possessions and spent what money they had to buy space for their families on tiny boats. Each boat was packed with people. It set sail in the hope of being picked

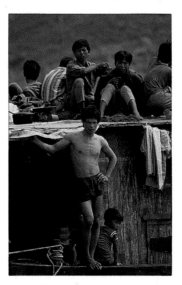

up by larger boats from other countries willing to help. One and a half million people have left Vietnam since the war ended in 1975.

Some countries have allowed the refugees to stay. Others have let them stay in special camps. Some have forced them to return to Vietnam. The Vietnamese boat people were so desperate to leave that they were prepared to gamble with their lives. Not all the small boats were rescued and many people drowned in their attempt to look for a new and better life.

◄ POOR ENTERPRISE

Every large city attracts people who have no land or money. These people survive by collecting other people's rubbish and recycling, or perhaps repairing it. This gives them a chance to make some money. Outside Manila, the capital of the Philippines, is Smoky Mountain, a huge rubbish dump. The dump is a source of income for many of the poorest city people.

People who have no steady work are often good at creating their own opportunities. In Indonesia, people pulled three-wheeled cabs called becaks. These were cheap alternatives to more usual taxis. But in 1989 this form of transport was banned by the Indonesian government, forcing 100,000 people to look for another way to earn money.

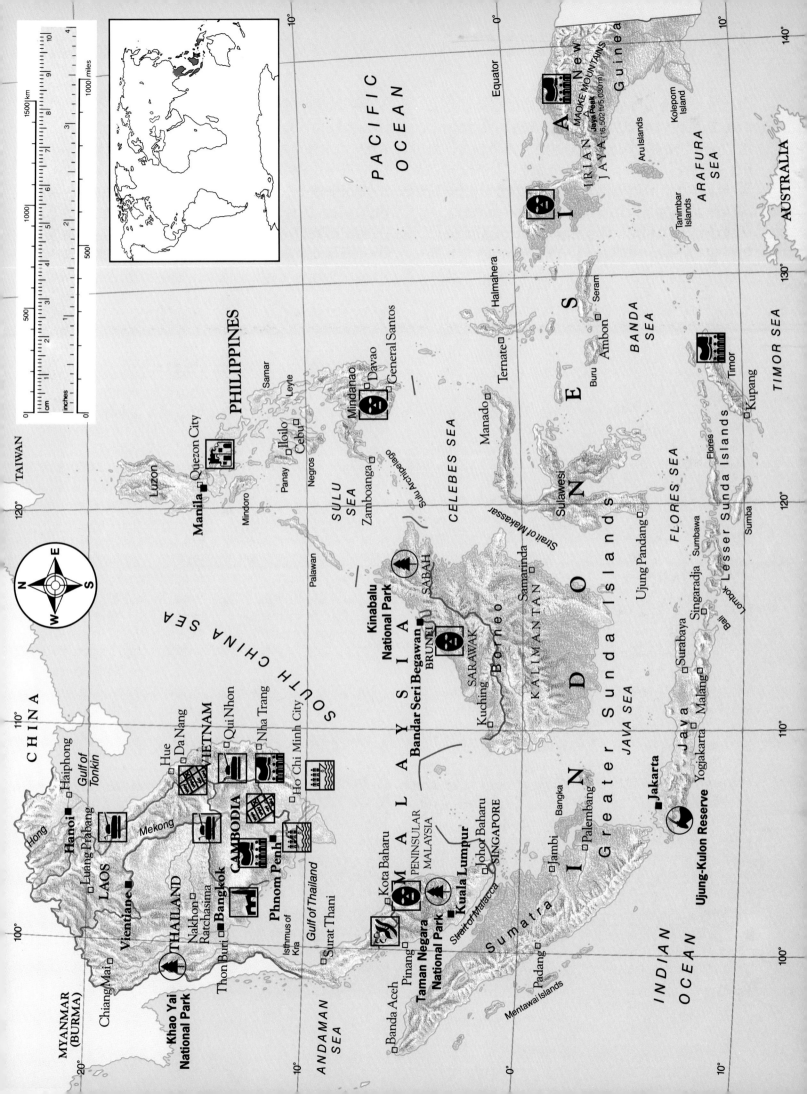

AUSTRALIA AND NEW ZEALAND

Australia is a vast, flat country. It has a population of 15 million. Most people live in towns and cities around the coast, and the interior is largely empty. The climate is very dry in most places, and there are large areas of desert or semi-desert. Rainfall is never regular and bushfires are a constant threat. The islands of New Zealand are a complete contrast.

They have regular rainfall and are mountainous in places. Australia was first colonised about 40,000 years ago. People came from the north-west, travelling by sea. New Zealand was colonised by Polynesians who came from islands in the Pacific Ocean about 1,000 years ago. Europeans did not settle in these lands until the eighteenth century.

▲ ABORIGINES

The original inhabitants of Australia came under great threat when European settlers first arrived in the late eighteenth century. The first Europeans settled in the south-east and south-west of the country. There, traditional ways of life were lost as the aborigine population became influenced by the settlers. In the centre and the north of the country some aboriginal groups were left undisturbed for much longer. They were semi-nomadic hunter-gatherers whose way of life fitted in perfectly with the dry, desert conditions.

The number of aborigines in Australia today is increasing. There are now about 250,000. Many depend on money from the state to live. There have been many demonstrations for the right to live in their way on the land. These have been quite successful. This has enabled some to return to their semi-nomadic way of life and helped to keep alive their culture and traditions.

▼ BUSHFIRES

Australia suffers from long-term drought. Often very little rain falls for years on end. Fire is therefore a serious risk. People and homes are especially threatened when fires break out near towns and cities. This happened in 1994, when bushfires reached the outskirts of Sydney, Australia's largest city, where more than 3.5 million people live.

MAORIS

Today, there are 300,000 Maoris in New Zealand, living mainly on the North Island. They make up about ten per cent of the population. Their language is related to Polynesian and they probably first came to New Zealand in the twelfth century. About three quarters of Maoris today are unemployed town dwellers.

Many Maoris have become increasingly involved in demanding land rights and political equality with European settlers. At present Maoris own about four per cent of the land, but they claim the right to about 70 per cent. The Waitanga Treaty in 1840 gave the British all the land and power and led to the Maori Wars (1860 –1872). Today, the Maoris want the treaty reviewed and their language to be officially recognised.

THE PACIFIC ISLANDS

Groups of people who may have come from China or Formosa reached these islands about 5,000 years ago. They moved from island to island. There is a remarkable similarity today between the islanders. They settled on Fiji, Samoa, Tonga, Easter Island and Hawaii. The people on many of these islands are dependent on fishing. The volcanic soil is very fertile but also very scarce.

▼ EXPLOITED ISLANDERS

From the sixteenth century onwards Europeans brought diseases against which the islanders had no natural resistance. Two thirds of the population of two islands, Tubuai and Raivavae, died in an epidemic brought by a visiting ship. The islanders' values and way of life were changed by missionaries. Some were transported to Fiji and Australia to work on cotton plantations for very low wages. Europeans exploited the islands by making one crop or resource important on each island so it could be traded on the international market.

▲ EASTER ISLAND

This island is made up of three extinct volcanoes. Its first inhabitants probably arrived almost 2,000 years ago. They left behind some amazing statues, which are up to 11 metres high and 45 tonnes in weight. About 600 have so far been excavated.

The islanders cut down trees so they could move the statues. Once the trees were gone, the soil blew away and the land became barren. The people then moved to another island where they could grow crops.

▼ NUCLEAR TESTS

This region of the world has been used by many different countries for **nuclear testing**. Nuclear weapons have been tested there since the mid-1940s.

Particular parts of the region, such as Bikini Atoll, have been contaminated with radiation from nuclear explosions.

During the early days of nuclear testing, scientists knew less about the effects of radiation. As a result, there were fewer safeguards and many people's lives were put at risk.

Today, most people believe that the threat of a war involving nuclear weapons is much smaller than it was because of the break-up of the former USSR.

A South Pacific nuclear-free zone treaty, called the Treaty of Rarotonga, was signed in 1985 and enforced in 1986.

THE ARCTIC

Centred on the North Pole, this region includes the Arctic Ocean, many islands and parts of North America, Russia and Scandinavia. Because of its extremely cold, dry climate it has always been sparsely populated. Today about 600,000 people live there. The original inhabitants were the Inuit of northern Canada, Alaska and Greenland and the Lapps in northern Scandinavia, who lived by hunting, fishing and herding reindeer for hundreds of years. Several hundred species of plants are to be found in the region, and many different animals.

▼ A MELTING TUNDRA?

Scientists are worried that the average temperature of the Earth will increase because of a build up of gases in the atmosphere. This would have a serious effect on the tundra, the frozen part of the Arctic, which covers 15 per cent of the Earth's surface. If there was global warming this permanent band of ice might melt and destroy the Arctic environment altogether. It would also release vast amounts of methane gas, which would make the global warming even worse.

▲ MINERAL WEALTH FOR ALL

There are enormous amounts of minerals in this region. Two thirds of Russia's gas reserves are north of the Arctic Circle. Alaska supplies a quarter of all the USA's oil needs. But the vast amounts of minerals in the Arctic have created problems not only for the natural environment but for the people who live in the region.

The discovery of oil in Alaska in 1968 started the USA's environmental and indigenous groups rights movement. The building of the Alaskan oil pipeline had to take into account the interests of the local people, who fought to be heard. Eventually they were given about 12 per cent of the land in Alaska and paid a billion dollars in cash. Since the agreement to build the pipeline, the population in the region has doubled and most of the state's income is from oil. These changes have affected the native people's way of life.

THE ANTARCTIC

This largely unexplored continent is about twice the size of Australia and has about ten per cent of all the land on Earth. There are no indigenous people. There has not been much human influence in the region, so it is relatively unpolluted. At any one time there are no more than 4,000 people living there.

These are mostly research scientists from various different countries. The Antarctic continent offers a chance for all countries to work together to achieve common aims. These aims are to understand better how the natural environment works and to carry out co-operative research.

OZONE DANGER ▶

In 1982, a team from the British Antarctic Survey discovered that much of the layer of ozone gas above the South Pole had disappeared. The thin band of ozone wrapped around the Earth's atmosphere cuts down the amount of **ultraviolet radiation** which reaches the Earth's surface.

Any increase in the radiation getting through the ozone layer would be harmful to all living things. It can lead to eye damage and an increase in skin cancer. Higher ultraviolet radiation would also damage plants and the food web in the oceans. This would increase the damage to the environment. Countries are trying to agree on how much they need to reduce the release of gases, including **CFCs**, which destroy the ozone layer.

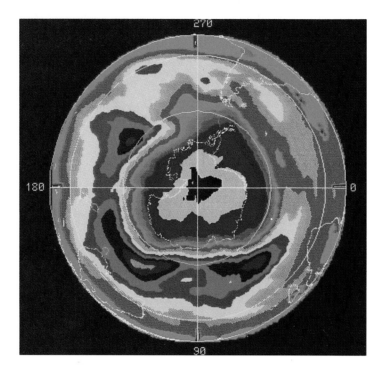

THE ANTARCTIC TREATY ▼

In 1961 the Antarctic treaty was signed by 12 nations recognising the great importance of this special environment. Since that time, many other countries have signed the treaty, and it was reviewed and extended in 1991. It aims to ensure peaceful research.

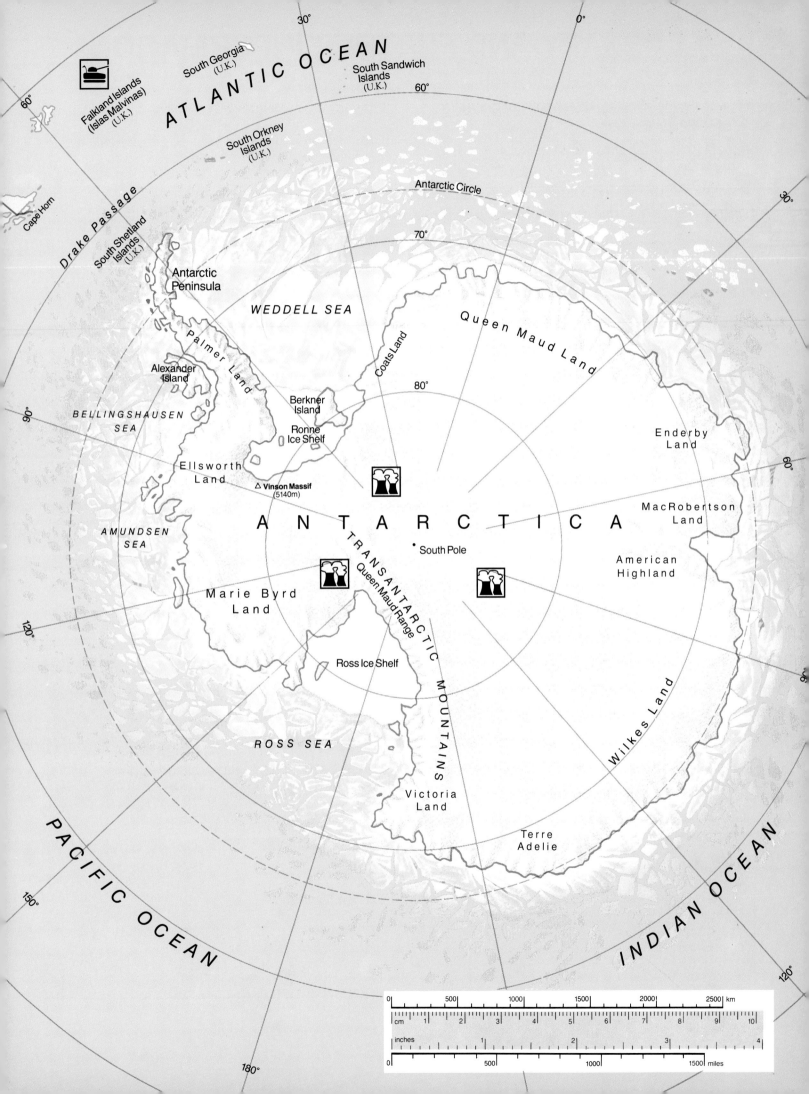

GLOSSARY AND FURTHER INFORMATION

Here are some simple explanations of the main terms used in this book.

Algal blooms Large collections of plants called algae that feed on pollution and spread rapidly. As the algae dies it rots, which uses up oxygen in the water and allows poisons to build up.

Apartheid An oppressive system that separated white people from black people in South Africa.

Blood fluke A microscopic creature that lives inside another animal's body as a parasite.

CFCs Chlorofluorocarbons (CFCs) are chemicals that are used in many modern processes from air conditioning to aerosol cans. They do not change, but remain for a long time in the atmosphere. They damage the ozone layer.

Cultivators People who grow, harvest and store crops. They are less dependent than hunter-gatherers on natural changes in their environment because food is available all year round.

Drainage patterns The way in which water runs off land into rivers and underground. This is affected by man-made and natural conditions.

Epidemics Diseases that spread quickly among people or animals. They are especially dangerous where there are poor living conditions.

Hunter-gatherers People who hunt wild animals and gather wild plants. They have no control over their environment but understand how to get what they need from it.

Hydroelectricity The use of falling water to drive machinery, which makes electricity.

Immunity A natural resistance to disease.

Industrial economies The term used to describe the way some countries make their money. They use raw materials to make goods that they sell around the world.

Intensive farming A method of farming that relies heavily on chemicals, such as pesticides, herbicides and fertilisers, to increase production of a single crop or of livestock.

Monsoon The rainy season in Asia and the Far East. In tropical areas it often rains very heavily every day for several weeks.

Nuclear testing The process in which nuclear bombs are exploded as an experiment.

Subsistence A way of life where people grow just enough food from the land to survive.

Topsoil The layer of soil that lies at the surface.

Ultraviolet radiation A form of radiation from the sun that is harmful to living things. The ozone layer protects the Earth from large amounts of ultraviolet radiation.

Vaccination The name given to a tiny dose of a disease, given to people to help them build up an immunity against it.

Water table The level at which water lies on the land. It may be below or at soil level. At times of drought or when farmers take too much water, the water table drops.

World market A term that refers to countries that trade their goods with each other all over the world. There is no one place where this happens.

FURTHER INFORMATION

Here is a selection of organisations that are actively involved in helping people all over the world whose environment or well-being is threatened. You can write to these organisations for further information.

Survival International
310 Edgware Road
London W2 1DY

Worldwide Fund For Nature
Panda House
Weyside Park
Godalming
Surrey GU7 1XR

Centre for World Development
Regent's College
Inner Circle
Regent's Park
London NW1 4NS

Cultural Survival UK
4 Albion Place
Galena Road
London W6 0LT

Oxfam
274 Banbury Road
Oxford OX2 7DZ

Friends of the Earth
26-28 Underwood Street
London N1 7JQ

MAP INDEX

INDEX OF PEOPLES AND THREATS TO THE ENVIRONMENT